THOMAS EDISON

A LERNER BIOGRAPHY

THOMAS EDISON

INVENTOR OF THE AGE OF ELECTRICITY

LINDA TAGLIAFERRO

LERNER PUBLICATIONS COMPANY / MINNEAPOLIS

*I would like to thank Doug Tarr, archivist at the Edison
National Historic Site for his generous help with this book.*

Lerner Publications Company
A division of Lerner Publishing Group
241 First Avenue North
Minneapolis, MN 55401 U.S.A.

Website address: www.lernerbooks.com

Library of Congress Cataloging-in-Publication Data

Tagliaferro, Linda.
    Thomas Edison : inventor of the age of electricity / by Linda
Tagliaferro.
        p.   cm. — (Lerner biographies)
    Summary: A biography of Thomas Alva Edison, the inventor of
the electric lighting system and the phonograph.
    Includes bibliographical references and index.
        ISBN: 0–8225–4689–2 (lib. bdg. : alk. paper)
        1. Edison, Thomas A. (Thomas Alva), 1847–1931—Juvenile
literature. 2. Inventors—United States—Biography—Juvenile
literature. 3. Electric engineers—United States—Biography—
Juvenile literature. [1. Edison, Thomas A. (Thomas Alva),
1847–1931. 2. Inventors.] I. Title.
TK140.E3 T35 2003
621.3'092—dc21   2002007603

Manufactured in the United States of America
1 2 3 4 5 6 – JR – 08 07 06 05 04 03

Contents

On New Year's Eve 1879, Thomas Alva Edison welcomed visitors to his Menlo Park laboratory to witness the miracle of electric lights.

ONE

The Seventh Child

On a dark winter night in Menlo Park, New Jersey, a curious crowd of three thousand people gathered in front of a group of laboratory buildings. It was New Year's Eve, 1879, and extra trains had been routed to the quiet town for a very special event. Thomas Edison, a young inventor, had promised to do something that most people considered impossible.

Excited visitors had been heading to Edison's laboratory in Menlo Park for days. Was the inventor telling the truth, they wondered, or was this just a publicity stunt? While they wondered, the long-awaited moment arrived.

The Menlo Park laboratory suddenly burst into light as electricity flowed through the many bulbs that had been installed there. Magically, with the flip of a switch, the rooms had been transformed from dark as night to light-filled day. On that stormy winter evening, as the old year was departing, Thomas Edison's guests were not only ushering in a new year. Edison's demonstration gave the promise of an entirely new era: the Age of Electricity. He had successfully invented the first practical lightbulb.

Unknown to the astounded crowds, this was just the beginning. Thomas Edison, the man who became known as the Wizard of Menlo Park, would go on to invent even more marvels. He would receive patents on more than one thousand inventions in his lifetime. He would live to see the phonograph, the motion picture industry, the electric lighting industry, and much more—he would change people's lives forever.

* * * *

It was an exciting time of growth for America when Thomas Alva Edison was born on February 11, 1847, in the little town of Milan, Ohio. James Polk had been elected president of the United States two years earlier, and by 1846, the country comprised twenty-nine states and a number of territories.

Times were very different then. Most Americans lived and worked on farms. Women were not allowed to vote in political elections. All of the slaves in the United States wouldn't be officially freed until the 13th Amendment was added to the Constitution in 1865. There were no telephones, electric appliances, or electric lighting. Homes and businesses were illuminated by the flickering flames of gaslights. The first railroad had been established in 1830, but many people still traveled by stagecoach.

The Edison family had originally emigrated from Holland in the early 1700s, when the present-day United States was a British colony. During the years before the American Revolution, when colonists fought for their independence, some people like John Edison, the great-grandfather of Thomas Edison, remained loyal to England. Many of those who were faithful to the British were forced to leave, and in 1773, John fled to Canada with his family.

Samuel Edison Jr., left, *and Nancy Edison,* right, *were Al Edison's parents.*

When John's grandson Samuel Jr. reached manhood, he married schoolteacher Nancy Elliott. In 1838 Samuel Jr. was involved with the losing side in a Canadian rebellion, and he, like his grandfather before him, was forced to leave his country.

Samuel Jr. chose to settle in Milan, Ohio, in the United States. Milan's canal linked it with Lake Erie, and the town became prosperous as a shipping center for grain transported through the Erie Canal to the eastern parts of the country.

Samuel Jr. and Nancy had seven children, but three died as infants. The last born was Thomas Alva Edison. His family and friends called him Al. When Al was born, he had two sisters, Marion and Harriet Ann, and a brother, William Pitt. All of them were teenagers at the time, so Al must have felt like an only child, surrounded by much older siblings and adults.

Al's birthplace in Milan, Ohio, has become a museum dedicated to his life.

Having lost three children, Nancy was especially attentive to her youngest child.

When Al was only two years old, his sister Marion married and left home to live with her husband. The little boy was brokenhearted and cried at the loss of his sister's constant companionship. William Pitt eventually spent more and more time with his younger brother.

One of Al's earliest memories was the sight of the covered wagons that stopped in front of his home. The Gold Rush started in 1849 when the precious metal was discovered in California. Adventurous people set out with high hopes and all their belongings in horse- or ox-drawn wagons to seek their fortune in the West.

When young Al was five, he went on his first vacation with his family. They sailed across Lake Erie to visit family members still living in Canada. The gathering was a great deal of fun for Al, especially when some of his relatives taught him how to swim. This skill saved his life a short time later, because Al, like many of the children raised in Milan, once accidentally fell into the canal.

Another boy in Milan was not so lucky. On one occasion, when Al and one of his playmates were exploring the Milan canal together, Al decided to jump into the water. The other boy followed his lead, but unfortunately, didn't know how to swim. Al panicked when he saw the boy's head go underwater. He didn't know what he should do, so he ran away from the canal and returned home in fright. He was very quiet when he greeted his parents and was too shaken to mention the incident. Shortly after coming home, Al went to his room. He went straight to bed and quivered under the covers.

Later that night, his friend's distraught parents came to the Edison home to inquire about their son. They had become

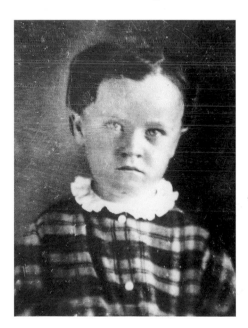

As a child, Al was active and curious.

frantic when their son hadn't returned, and they knew that he had been playing with the young Edison boy. Al's family woke him up and questioned him. Only then did the frightened youngster reveal the events that had taken the life of his friend.

As a child, Al had a sharp mind and an active curiosity. He constantly asked questions of anyone within earshot. If his father honestly told the boy that he didn't know the answers to his queries, Al would lose patience, demanding, "Why don't you know?"

This curiosity sometimes led Al into trouble. Once it led him to experiment with ways to light a fire, and he learned all too well. He accidentally set fire to his father's barn, and the flames spread until the entire building burned down. Al was lucky to escape the blaze, but he didn't escape his father's wrath. Furious at losing an entire barn, Samuel Jr. gave his son a beating in the middle of the town square, where all the passersby could see.

Although Al had a strong mind, his body was not so hardy. He caught scarlet fever, a serious disease that brings a sore throat, high fever, and a deep red rash to its victims, and he was plagued by frequent bouts of colds and other respiratory illnesses, especially during Ohio's cold winters.

When Al was seven years old, the business boom in Milan had slowed, so Samuel Jr. decided to move to thriving Port Huron, Michigan. The Edison family settled into a comfortable large house surrounded by apple and pear trees.

Al was enrolled in the local public school, but his curiosity and constant questions annoyed the teacher. Al said that he was always "at the foot of the class," and he only attended the school for about three months. Then Nancy Edison took

When he was eight, Al posed for a photo with his sister Harriet Ann. His brother and two sisters were teenagers when he was born.

him out and taught him at home, where he acquired a great deal of knowledge on his own.

Young Al was so grateful to his mother for her strong confidence in him that he was determined not to let her down. "I felt that I had someone to live for," he said, "someone I must not disappoint."

He certainly didn't disappoint her in his studies at home. Reading was one of his favorite activities. By the time Al was nine years old, he had read many adult books including Hume's *History of England,* Gibbon's *The Decline and Fall of the Roman Empire,* and Sears's *History of the World.* He also read a number of books on electricity. The boy had a remarkable memory, and he easily remembered what he read.

A few years later, he read the writings of Thomas Paine, whose books inspired the patriots of the American Revolution. He also read *Principia,* by Sir Isaac Newton, the acclaimed British mathematician. As an adult, Al said that Newton's book gave him "a distaste for mathematics."

Science fascinated Al's curious mind. He was living at a time of breakthrough discoveries in science. In the early 1800s, scientists were unraveling the secrets of electricity and magnetism. Hans Christian Oersted in Denmark, and later André-Marie Ampère in France discovered that an electric current sent through a wire exerted the same kind of force as a magnet. American physicist Joseph Henry created the first useful electric motor.

In 1844, just three years before Al was born, Samuel Morse, an American artist and inventor, had patented the telegraph, a device that could send messages to faraway places through metal wires. These messages were sent in a special code made up of dots and dashes—short and long electric impulses—representing letters and numbers.

Samuel Morse invented the telegraph, which sent messages over wires to distance places.

Morse's telegraph sent its messages as a series of different long and short electric impulses, called dots and dashes, for each letter. This chart shows letters translated into the dots and dashes of Morse code.

Morse's telegraph revolutionized long distance communication. Before the telegraph, letters carried by horseback or ship were the main ways people communicated when they were apart. All of a sudden, speedy messages were possible over long distances.

When Al was nine years old, he read a science textbook, Richard Green Parker's *Natural and Experimental Philosophy*. This was one of the books that spurred his great interest in science. Al set up a laboratory in his family's basement in the 1850s. Not content to believe everything that he read, Al personally tested all the experiments in this book. He collected bottles and filled them with various chemicals. He labeled them all "Poison" and systematically arranged them on shelves.

Al sometimes came up with false conclusions. He convinced a gullible friend of his to swallow a large amount of Seidlitz powders—a type of laxative—by convincing him that it would enable him to fly. Al knew that some gases are lighter than air and concluded that the Seidlitz powders would generate gases that would enable his friend to float.

When Al's ill-fated experiment was carried out, all it resulted in was a severe stomachache for his hapless friend. Tom's mother was furious, and he was punished for endangering the health of his companion.

Nancy Edison also worried that her boy would one day accidentally blow up the house, but the eager young scientist

The Grand Trunk Railroad connected Canada and the United States over this bridge on the Niagara River. In 1859 the rail line built tracks to link Al's hometown of Port Huron, Michigan, to Detroit.

continued collecting chemicals and mixing them together. Al's curiosity, remarkable memory, and perseverance were his most notable characteristics as a child, and these traits followed him into adulthood.

When Al turned twelve, he longed to become more independent and to explore the world beyond his town. In 1859 the Grand Trunk Railroad built tracks to connect Port Huron to Detroit. Al convinced his mother and father that he was a capable young man who could earn his own money for the supplies for his experiments. In those times, it was not unusual for boys to go to work, and with his parents' permission, he eagerly applied for employment on the railroad.

Al at fourteen, when he worked as a candy butcher

Two

The Candy Butcher

It must have been an exciting day for twelve-year-old Thomas Alva Edison when he first stepped aboard a Grand Trunk Railroad train as an employee. Al was what they called a candy butcher—someone who sold candy, dried fruits, newspapers, books, and other items to passengers. He boarded the 7 A.M. train from Port Huron with his wares, and four hours later, after a number of stops along the route, he arrived in Detroit.

The train didn't immediately turn back to Port Huron. Al had to wait until 5:30 in the afternoon for his return trip, and he didn't get home until 9:30 at night. But the curious youngster welcomed this extra time to explore.

Al took advantage of his extended daytime break to visit the Detroit Public Library. Eager to learn about almost any subject, he read his way through as many sections as possible during his long visits. His plan was to choose one section at a time and then to read each and every book on the shelves in that area.

It was around this time that it became clear that Al was going deaf. There are many theories about how and why he lost most of his hearing. It might have been from his series of childhood illnesses, including the scarlet fever. Or it may have happened when an enraged stationmaster hit Al on the ear. Another theory holds that his hearing difficulties stemmed from the time that he was delayed by newspaper customers at one of the stations and had to run to catch the departing train. He had finally just managed to catch onto the back of the moving train, and a worker helped him by reaching down and pulling him up by the ears. Edison once said that if this man had indeed caused a hearing injury with this action, it was while he was moving quickly to save the young man from falling off the speeding train and onto the tracks.

Although many people would consider a loss of hearing to be a great disadvantage, Al turned it into an advantage. He once commented that his hearing difficulties actually made it easier for him to concentrate even when he was in noisy surroundings. Even when his hearing became worse later in his life, he never lost the ability to converse with people when they spoke closely into his ears.

Al's job not only gave him a big daytime break in Detroit, where he spent many hours in the new public library, it also gave him free time after he had sold his wares on the train. One of the baggage cars had a small compartment that was empty. Al was told that he could use it as a storage space for his stock of newspapers and all of the other items that he sold to the passengers. He took the contents of his laboratory out of his family's basement and stacked them on the shelves of the empty baggage car. Al spent many hours experimenting when his work on the train was done, or when he had the layover in Detroit.

Candy butchers did not make a great deal of money, but Al found ways to supplement his modest income. When he

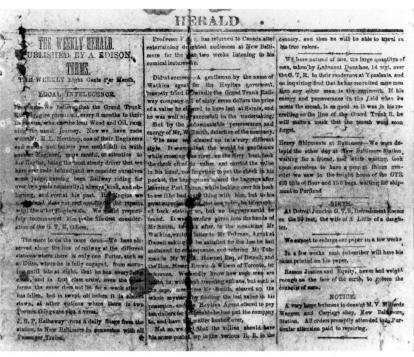

The first newspaper printed on a moving train. Al wrote and printed the Weekly Herald in the baggage car that also held his chemistry laboratory.

was fourteen, he purchased a small printing press and stored it in his space in the baggage car. He wrote and printed the *Weekly Herald,* which he claimed was the first newspaper printed on a moving train. The newspaper featured local news and changes in the train schedules along the Port Huron–Detroit line. Al sold the paper for three cents. Hundreds of copies were printed each week, and Al sometimes made as much as twenty to thirty dollars a month for his efforts.

In addition, after Al had worked on the train for a few months, he started two stores in Port Huron. One was for magazines and newspapers, and the other one offered fresh produce, including the vegetables and berries that were grown on the family's land.

After an express train was added to the line that Al worked on, he had the opportunity to buy produce in Detroit and expand the variety of foods that he offered in his store. Every day he would buy two large baskets with an assortment of vegetables at wholesale prices from the vegetable market in Detroit and bring them onboard the train. When Al arrived in Port Huron, he would carry them over to his store.

Al also stopped at various stations along the line and purchased fresh butter from the farmers who lived there. By purchasing these goods directly from farmers, Al bought them at low prices and made a handsome profit when he sold the produce and butter at higher prices.

Al hired two young boys to run the stores for him, and the three took equal shares of the profits they made from sales. The vegetable store remained open for almost a year.

Occasionally, Al would also make money by delivering messages. One of the largest steamboat companies operating on the Great Lakes in the mid-1800s was E. B. Ward & Company. When the captain of one of their largest boats suddenly died, the company needed to send a message immediately to another captain to take his place. Al was recruited to make a fourteen-mile journey on foot from one of the stations on his line to the home of the captain.

Al had been forewarned that the road leading to the captain's house passed through dark, deserted stretches of forest. He decided to take another boy along with him, and the two set out with lanterns to light their way in the darkness.

It was raining when they began their journey at 8:30 in the evening. The two boys were frightened for many reasons. They were alone on a cold, black night, they could barely see where they were going, and they knew that wild animals roamed freely through the area. Al was especially afraid of encounters with bears in the forest. As the two boys made their way through the spooky surroundings, their imaginations started to run wild. The gnarled tree stumps that stood before them in the darkness began to look like bears. When Al's companion begged him to seek refuge on the higher branches of a tree to escape from any bears that might be prowling in the forest, Al told him that it wouldn't do any good because the animals knew how to climb.

To make matters worse, one of the lanterns suddenly went out. Shortly afterward, the second lantern was extinguished. The two frightened boys started to cry but were determined to find their way out of the forest. They stayed on the path and eventually found the house of the captain and delivered their message just as the sun was coming up.

In 1861 the Civil War had begun and would continue to rage on until 1865. In those days, it took a long time for people to get news. There were no telephones, televisions, or radios to quickly spread the latest developments of the war. The telegraph was the fastest means of communication, and newspaper news bureaus were set up to receive telegraphed reports. People eagerly awaited the most up-to-date information in the newspapers.

On April 6, 1862, a great battle erupted at Shiloh in Tennessee. The opposing armies headed by Confederate (Southern) general Albert Johnston and Union (Northern) general Ulysses S. Grant had clashed, and more than twenty thousand people were killed or wounded.

When Al arrived in Detroit on that April day, he went as usual to pick up his supply of the *Detroit Free Press,* the main newspaper he sold to passengers on his route. As soon as he

A bloody Civil War battle was fought at Shiloh, and customers along Al's route clamored for news of it.

heard the news of the battle, he decided to ask for one thousand papers to sell on the train instead of his usual one hundred copies.

Then he went to a local telegraph operator and persuaded him to telegraph the headlines about the bloody battle to all the train stations in the small towns along Al's route, in turn promising him free newspapers for the next three months. The teenager hoped that this would whet the interest of people along the route and persuade them to buy the paper and read the detailed reports of the Battle of Shiloh. People with relatives serving as soldiers desperately longed for any news about them.

When the train arrived at Utica, Michigan, the first stop after Detroit, Al was surrounded by crowds of people who were eager for news of the battle. He usually only sold two papers at that stop, but on that April day, he sold thirty-five for five cents apiece. At the next stop, Al doubled the price of the newspaper to ten cents. When the train reached Port Huron, Al sold the remainder of his papers for twenty-five cents each.

Al was good at managing his profits and even gave some money to his mother. He spent most of his earnings on his laboratory's stock of chemicals. He continually added to the shelves that were reserved for him in the empty baggage car and spent many hours conducting chemical experiments during his free time on the train.

Once more his curiosity got him into trouble. One day the train went through a badly constructed stretch of tracks while Al was experimenting in his baggage compartment lab. As the train pitched forward, one of the bottles of chemicals flew off the shelf onto the floor and caught fire.

This replica of Al's baggage car shows the chemical laboratory where he conducted chemical experiments.

Al couldn't control the flames, but Alexander Stevenson, the conductor, burst into the car and put the fire out. At the very next stop, Mount Clemens, the angry conductor ordered Al off the train and threw all his bottles onto the platform with him. Then he hurled out Al's printing press and anything else that he could find that belonged to the unlucky experimenter.

Later that year, Al's luck took a turn for the better. Stationmaster James MacKenzie's young son was sitting on the railroad tracks playing with pebbles and didn't notice an oncoming train. Risking his own life, Al pulled the child off the tracks to safety. MacKenzie was so grateful to the heroic teenager that he offered to teach him telegraphy, a skill that was as important then as advanced computer skills later

Al rescued the son of the stationmaster at the Mount Clemens station.

James MacKenzie, the Mount Clemens stationmaster, taught Al how to operate the telegraph.

became. In the fall of 1863, he went even further in thanking Al. He helped to get the teenager a telegrapher's job in Canada, at the Stratford, Ontario, railroad station.

Al was excited to take on this new responsibility. It was the first of a series of jobs that would take him on adventures around the country as a roving tramp telegrapher—a traveling worker who took jobs whenever and wherever services were needed.

Civil War news, sent directly from the front lines by telegraphers like this one in a tent in Virginia, created a great need all over the country for telegraph operators to receive and pass on the news to the people at home.

THREE

The Tramp Telegrapher

Al Edison was sixteen when he joined the ranks of tramp telegraphers, wandering from city to city to fill jobs as they became available. Adventurous young men could earn a living and develop their skills while exploring new parts of the country. Often train conductors allowed them to ride the trains for free.

There were certainly many jobs for telegraphers. The Civil War created a great demand for skilled telegraph operators, not only for military purposes, but also for civilian business. For the five-year period from 1863 until 1868, Al was a tramp telegrapher in Canada and places throughout the Midwest including Michigan, Indiana, Ohio, and Kentucky.

Al was home during the severe winter of 1863–1864 when ice filled the river that flowed between Port Huron, Michigan, and Sarnia, Canada, and broke the telegraphic cable connection between the two towns. While others wondered what to do to fix the cable, Al's inventive mind went to work.

A locomotive was standing near the riverbank in Port Huron. Pulling on the cord that set off the train's loud whistle, Al controlled the length of his tugs to produce whistle blasts that resembled the dots and dashes of Morse code. More than a mile away, telegraph operators in Sarnia understood the message and soon replied with their own locomotive whistles. Messages were sent this way until the cable could be repaired.

Al's ingenuity still could get him into trouble from time to time. Trouble came while Al was working in Canada as a telegraph operator on the night shift.

During the day, he worked on his own experiments instead of catching up on his sleep. At night, on the job, he was required to send a special telegraphic signal every half hour to the train dispatcher at a nearby station to show that he was alert and ready to take down messages. This, of course, interfered with Al's stolen naps, but he devised an ingenious way of hooking up his telegraph machine to a clock so that the signal was automatically sent out. After setting up the device, he dozed off in peace.

One night, the train dispatcher decided to have a friendly chat with Al over the telegraph wires. When there was no answer, he took off for the station to see what was wrong. He found the teenager sleeping soundly, while the hands of the clock quietly moved to the half hour and set off Al's telegraphic invention. Furious at Al's deception, the dispatcher woke the startled young man out of his deep sleep and fired him on the spot.

Al moved to Cincinnati, Ohio, in 1865, where he made friends with several other telegraph operators. Shakespeare's plays were extremely popular in the United States at that time, and Al and his new friend, Ezra Gilliland, frequented the local theater to see performances.

Ezra and Al worked on increasing their telegraphic skills by sending each other the scripts of the plays through Morse code. Al also memorized some of the lines and would

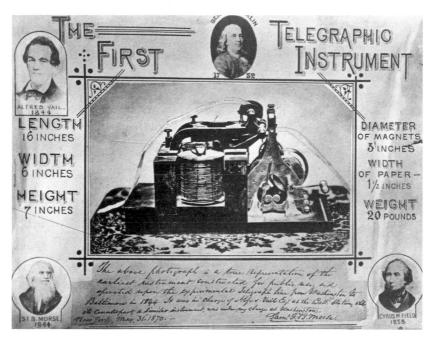

This original telegraph, invented by Samuel Morse, is similar to telegraphs Edison used in his years as a tramp telegrapher.

amuse his coworkers with exaggerated impersonations of Shakespearean characters.

During his years as a tramp operator, Al continued to experiment and to read voraciously. His years of studying at home with his mother had taught him the value of self-education. He kept detailed notebooks with diagrams and descriptions of his many inventive ideas. He often visited secondhand bookstores to find books about subjects he was interested in. His coworkers nicknamed him Victor Hugo Edison because they often found him reading the novels of Victor Hugo, the French author.

One night Al was hurrying home at 3 A.M. after working on the night shift, carrying the heavy load of his latest book-buying spree. Suddenly, a shot rang out and something

When he worked in the Boston office of Western Union, Al sent and received messages from the New York office, pictured here.

whizzed by close to his head. A policeman had become suspicious when he saw a shadowy figure rushing through the streets with a load of goods on his back. He had called out a warning to stop, but since Al's hearing was poor, he had no idea that someone was pursuing him. When Al didn't answer, the policeman took out his gun and fired, narrowly missing him.

In 1868, when he was twenty-one, Al journeyed to Boston, Massachusetts, where he worked for Western Union, a well-known telegraph company. He was immediately assigned to take down the information sent by a telegrapher in New York. Al didn't realize that the other operators purposely waited for the fastest operator to test the new employee's speed. The messages came in a flood of dots and dashes, and initially Al had a hard time writing down all the words, but he managed to keep up the lightning pace.

Al turned around to find all the other operators watching him and eagerly waiting for him to give up. Eventually, the New York operator couldn't keep up his rapid pace, and Al broke in to wire him, "You seem to be tired, suppose you send a little while with your other foot." The other employees enjoyed Al's joke, and from then on they had a high regard for the new skilled worker.

Al worked nights at Western Union, and his days were reserved for his own experiments. He always had a number of projects going simultaneously. If he couldn't resolve one problem, he would move on to another project. Work on a second project often helped him to find the solution to the problems of the first one.

In 1868 Al perfected his first patented invention, the electric vote recorder, which was designed to make voting easier for legislators at congressional meetings. He was greatly disappointed when politicians rejected his idea. From that day

The vote recorder was Edison's first patented invention. It never caught on with politicians.

forward, Al resolved never to work on any invention unless there was a market for it.

Al journeyed once more in 1869, arriving penniless in New York City, the center of the U.S. telegraph industry. He was allowed to spend time in the Wall Street offices of the Gold and Stock Reporting Telegraph Company until he found a steady job. The company provided a service that sent the up-to-date prices of gold to its subscribers via a special telegraph transmitter.

One day, the transmitter broke down. Messengers from the company's subscribers came running into the main office, complaining that they weren't getting their service. No one in the company knew what to do, but Al went to work to try to fix the problem. He discovered a broken spring lodged between two gear wheels.

The owner of the company, Dr. Samuel Laws, immediately offered Al a job. A month later, he was promoted to superintendent, with a salary of three hundred dollars a month, an enormous amount for 1869. Soon after, though, Al resigned and started an electrical engineering firm with Franklin L. Pope, whom he had met while working at the Laws company.

One of Al and Franklin Pope's clients was Marshall Lefferts, the president of Western Union. Lefferts hired the firm to make improvements on the company's stock tickers, the telegraphic machine that transmitted stock prices to brokers and investors. Lefferts was greatly pleased with Al's invention, the Universal Stock Ticker, and asked him how much money he wanted for it. Al thought it was worth five thousand dollars, but he was afraid to ask for that much money, so he shyly asked Lefferts to make him an offer.

When Lefferts offered Al forty thousand dollars, the inventor was thunderstruck. When Al described this incident

Al was offered forty thousand dollars for the stock ticker he invented.

later, he commented, "I was afraid that [Lefferts] would hear my heart beat. I managed to say that I thought it was fair."

Al was financially independent, so he opened a factory in Newark, New Jersey. Here he began his longtime habit of working nearly twenty hours each day, interrupted only by brief naps on benches, tables, or the floor. Among his successes at this time were improvements in duplex telegraphy—which made it possible to send two messages simultaneously on one telegraph wire—and the invention of the quadruplex telegraph—which accommodated four simultaneous messages, two in each direction.

The happiness Al felt from the success of his inventions was interrupted by the death of his mother on April 9, 1871. Although deeply grieved by the loss, Al continued work on his many projects. Among these was his electric pen, which created a stencil to produce multiple copies of letters, long before the advent of photocopying machines. Al also helped

Edison opened this factory in Newark, New Jersey, to work on his inventions full time.

another inventor named Christopher L. Sholes improve his original typewriter so that it could be used successfully.

One day in 1871, while he was standing behind one of his employees, pretty sixteen-year-old Mary Stilwell, she turned to face him. She said that for some odd reason she always knew when he was standing near her. She asked him if he knew why.

Twenty-four-year-old Al Edison was a genius at inventing, but he wasn't a master of romance. He shyly said that he didn't know the answer to her question, but that he had been thinking a lot about her lately. Suddenly, he blurted out that he wanted to marry her.

Mary was shocked. Her boss had never even asked her out on a date. Al suggested that if Mary agreed, then they could be married shortly. He added, in an almost business-like tone, that he would like her answer as soon as possible. This sudden romance culminated in a wedding two weeks later, on Christmas Day, 1871.

Two years later, Mary gave birth to the Edisons' first child, Marion. In 1876 Thomas Alva Jr. was born. Al

This picture of Mary Stilwell Edison was taken around the time of her marriage to Al.

nicknamed them Dot and Dash after the Morse code symbols. Although Al loved his family, he devoted most of his time to his factory and his inventions and spent little time at home. Mary became depressed because she was alone for many hours while her husband toiled at his experiments.

For several years following his marriage, Al continued to manufacture telegraph instruments in his various shops. At one point, he traveled to England to introduce his improvements in telegraphy to Europe. Although the trip wasn't a financial success, he came home filled with ideas for new electrical experiments.

In 1876 Al decided to move his invention facilities from Newark to a more secluded place. He wanted to establish a large laboratory where his team could devote itself entirely to experiments. With profits from his manufacturing shops, Al built a well-equipped lab in the quiet town of Menlo Park, New Jersey. This would soon be the site of some of Al's greatest inventions.

Edison's laboratory in Menlo Park, New Jersey, was the first to employ team research.

FOUR

The Talking Machine

Al set up his new laboratory in Menlo Park as an "invention factory." In a way, this was one of his greatest inventions. Menlo Park was the first lab that employed team research. It served as an early model for modern-day research and development departments, where large corporations rely on teamwork to arrive at solutions to problems.

Before Menlo Park, inventors usually worked alone. But Al hand-picked employees with various important skills. Some were specialists in chemistry, others were experts in model making. The inventor would direct his men to tackle problems from different points of view. Each one's ideas would inspire the others.

At this time, the Edison family lived in Menlo Park. Daughter Marion was four, and Thomas Alva Jr. was three months old. Mary Edison felt displaced by the move, even though they owned an impressive house on a large plot of land surrounded by a white picket fence. Her family and friends were left behind in Newark, and her husband spent increasingly long hours at his new laboratory.

Mary Edison is standing on the porch of the Edisons' new home in Menlo Park, one block away from Al's laboratory.

Even though his workplace was just one block away from home, Al rarely ate with his family. When he was working on his inventions, he concentrated so deeply that he didn't think about other things. Even when he took breaks from work, he might go fishing with his employees instead of spending time with his wife and children.

It was clear that the inventor felt most at home in his lab. He loved putting in long, hard hours, and he enjoyed joking around in the all-male environment. His employees looked up to him and affectionately referred to him as the old man, even though he was only twenty-nine years old at the time.

Al and his employees often had dinner together in the lab late at night and sang songs while one of them played on the organ. Then they would resume their work and often didn't quit until early in the morning.

On these evenings, Al would send messages to Mary saying that he wouldn't be coming home because he was following up on a project. Mary was afraid to sleep alone in the isolated country village. To calm her fears, the inventor bought his wife a revolver, and she slept with it under her pillow.

Once Al did come home late at night. He walked through the door in his soiled clothes, and, too exhausted to make it to the bedroom, he went to sleep in the nearby guest room. The next morning, Mary found her husband in his filthy work clothes, curled up in a delicate white blanket.

One project that engaged Al at this time was work on the newly invented telephone. In 1876 Alexander Graham Bell developed the machine to carry voices over electric wires, but the original model was far from perfect. The president of Western Union hired Al to improve it.

Al developed a new type of transmitter, the part that sends out the telephone message. Al's new tranmitter was in

Edison improved Alexander Graham Bell's telephone by developing a new carbon transmitter.

the form of a carbon button. In successful tests, this transmitter allowed telephone conversations to be conducted between places as far away as New York and Philadelphia—a distance of more than one hundred miles. Al had figured out how to make Bell's invention a practical reality.

Edison believed strongly that even so-called failed experiments were really a learning process that helped him find the proper solution. Whatever didn't work could then be eliminated, and he could forge ahead and find out what steps would lead him to success.

One such accidental device turned out to be one of his most important inventions. Al had noticed that even the most gentle ocean waves leave an impression in the sand. He saw, too, that if a piano was played near a smooth plate of glass covered with a thin layer of sand, the musical sounds would rearrange the sand in specific patterns.

While trying to invent a device to automatically record telegraph messages, Al covered a revolving metal plate with a thin piece of paper. A needle mounted on an arm made impressions in the paper when the signals from the telegraph were received. These impressions could later be picked up by the needle attached to a receiver and the message repeated.

Al noticed a strange, unexpected result: humming sounds came out of the embossed paper when the needle attached to the receiver moved over the impressions. He thought the sounds resembled the muffled voices of people talking in the background and concluded that he might use the device to actually record sounds made by the human voice. But busy as usual, he went on to his other experiments and didn't return to his voice recording idea until months later.

The inventor kept highly detailed notebooks. One of them bears a sketch of his proposed idea for a speech

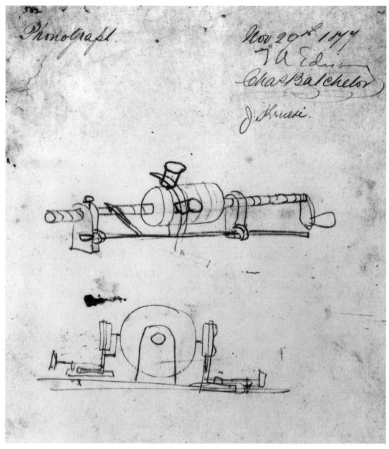

Edison drew sketches for his phonograph in the notebooks he kept to record his ideas and developments.

recorder. He named it the phonograph, from two Greek words meaning "sound writing." The original drawing shows a simple machine with a grooved cylinder wrapped in tin foil with a crank on its side.

A diaphragm, a piece of fabric stretched tight, would vibrate in response to sound waves. The diaphragm was attached to a sharply pointed needle. As it vibrated, the needle, vibrating along with it, created a patterned indentation in the tin foil. The louder someone spoke, Al reasoned, the farther the needle would be pushed into the tin foil, and the deeper the impression it would make.

In December 1877, Al gave his sketch to model-maker John Kruesi, who completed the machine according to the inventor's specifications. Al gathered some of his workers for the first test of his new device. None of them believed that he could record the sounds of a human voice. Neither did Al. He once remarked, "I didn't have much faith that it would work, expecting that I might possibly hear a word or so that would give hope of a future for the idea."

No one realized what a historic moment they were about to witness. The inventor turned the crank and recited the following familiar words into the receiver: "Mary had a little lamb. Its fleece was white as snow." The vibrating needle left impressions in the tin foil as Al spoke.

The first words recorded and played by Al's original phonograph, above, were, "Mary had a little lamb."

Then the inventor placed the needle on the newly inscribed tin foil "record" and turned the crank. What came out of the machine was the faint and scratchy, but unmistakable, sound of his voice. Everyone was astounded.

The very next day, Al and two assistants caused a stir in the offices of *Scientific American* magazine, where the editor and others were treated to a demonstration. To their amazement and delight, a recording asked how they were doing, mentioned that the machine itself felt just fine, and then politely said good night.

Rutherford B. Hayes, the president of the United States, heard about the demonstration, and invited Al to the White House one evening. The president was so taken with the invention that he woke up his wife so she could share in the

Edison, right, *was photographed with one of his associates, Charles Batchelor, when he demonstrated his phonograph at the offices of* Scientific American *magazine.*

enjoyment. Al and his invention entertained the first family until half past three in the morning.

The success of the phonograph made people around the world aware of Al's talents. One reporter dubbed him the Wizard of Menlo Park, and this description became one of Al's most famous nicknames.

Al continued to work on the phonograph, which he called his baby. He said that he expected it "to grow up to be a big feller" some day.

Al didn't develop his phonograph to bring musical entertainment into people's homes. He originally thought of his invention as a business tool. He envisioned bosses dictating letters into the machine, and later, their secretaries typing the letters while listening to the recordings. He never guessed that it would be the start of a music industry that continues to expand with modern innovations, like CDs and the CD player.

One hundred years after Edison's birth, students in West Orange, New Jersey, dance to recorded music next to a model of Edison's original phonograph, which made it all possible.

Al accompanied a group of scientists to Wyoming to study an eclipse of the Sun.

This discovery led to other, related inventions. Among these was the megaphone, a funnel-shaped device that made it possible for people to project their voices over long distances by speaking into a mouthpiece.

Although Al's work on perfecting the phonograph went on for many years, he experimented on other projects at the same time. Sometimes he would drop his work on the phonograph altogether for a period, then return to it. The method worked well for him and kept his mind busy acquiring information that he could use in any number of his projects.

Around this time, George F. Barker, a physician and friend of Al's, suggested that the inventor take a vacation. Barker invited Al to accompany him, along with physicist Henry Draper and a group of astronomers, on a trip to the Wyoming Territory. (Wyoming did not become a state until 1890.) Although Mary Edison was six months pregnant with their third child, the inventor agreed to travel because the Wyoming Territory promised to be a perfect spot to observe the upcoming eclipse of the Sun on July 29, 1878.

Al was eager to test one of his inventions, the tasimeter, which took extremely sensitive measurements of temperature.

The solar eclipse would provide Al with a unique opportunity to measure the drop in temperature when the Sun was in eclipse.

Although Al in the end was not satisfied with his tasimeter experiment, his trip was exciting and fruitful. After the eclipse, Al went hunting with Barker and others and traveled great distances by train. Along the way, Al had a spectacular up-close view of the scenery. He had received permission to sit on the locomotives' cowcatchers, the metal frames on the front of the train that pushed aside any stray objects that might be on the tracks. Sitting on a small cushion, Al rode the rails from Omaha, Nebraska, to the Sacramento Valley of California.

While the inventor was exploring the West, his wife was having a difficult pregnancy back home. Her doctor sent a

Al rode the cowcatcher of trains throughout the West to view the scenery, just as this group is doing at an earlier period in the eastern United States.

telegram to Al, asking him to return at once because Mary had fallen ill and was extremely nervous. He wired back to the doctor that he would return in a few days. But instead, he went to St. Louis, Missouri, to attend a scientific meeting, returning home to his pregnant wife six days after he received the doctor's urgent telegram.

When he arrived in his lab in late August 1878, Al was well rested and ready to tackle the business of inventing. But the commercial development of the phonograph was put on hold. By September Al was devoting most of his time to developing an invention that had eluded many of the scientists of the time.

*Edison was thirty-one when he announced that he would invent
the lightbulb and an electrical power system.*

FIVE

Lighting the World

In September 1878, Thomas Alva Edison, with swaggering self-confidence, announced to startled reporters that within six weeks, he and his team of workers would invent a practical electrical lightbulb and an electrical power system to go with it.

At the time, most people in cities illuminated their homes and offices with lamps that burned gas delivered to the premises by local gas companies. Gaslight provided only a soft, flickering glow, and it could be dangerous because the gas itself was both flammable and poisonous. If the flame went out and the gas spread into a room, it could result in the death of the people who inhaled it.

Since the mid-1800s, one type of electrical illumination, called arc lighting, had been available. The intense light was created by a spark of electricity that traveled between two carbon rods. Arc lighting was glaringly unpleasant and gave off poisonous fumes as it burned.

Al was sure that he could come up with something safer and more efficient if he experimented in a different direction. He would search for substances that could be subjected to

Al and some of his associates pose for the camera inside the Menlo Park lab.

very high temperatures and heated to incandescence—the point at which a substance glows with a steady white light.

Although a number of scientists around the world had attempted to produce an incandescent lamp, all of their efforts ended in only limited success or outright failure. Many scientists of the time had concluded that a practical incandescent light was impossible. But Al always believed that he could succeed at anything if he put his mind to it. So he assembled his team and hired a glassblower to craft the bulbs to house the many materials that would be tested for their ability to burn for long hours.

Al had been overly optimistic and a bit brash when he said he could succeed in six weeks. But he never became discouraged. One of the inventor's employees, Francis Upton, commented about his boss, "His greatness was always to be clearly seen when difficulties arose. They always made him cheerful, and started him thinking."

Al's hard work and unshakable optimism inspired everyone in the lab. If workers lost faith in their projects after repeated failures, Al reminded them that they had learned what didn't work. Then they could go in the right direction.

On October 26, 1878, shortly after Al embarked on his electric lighting experiments, Mary gave birth to their third child, William Leslie. Although proud to be a father one more time, Al was intensely busy in his laboratory, and Mary had to raise the three children mostly on her own.

From the outset of the lightbulb experiments, Al's greatest concern was to find the proper filament—the thin wire that would glow when an electric current was passed through it. He needed something that was strong enough to withstand the heat of the electric current without immediately burning out.

As usual, Al investigated materials in a very thorough, methodical way. He and his team first made filaments out of platinum. Eventually, after trying out a vast array of other

Al and Mary's three children: Marion, left, *Thomas Alva Edison Jr.,* center, *and William Leslie,* right

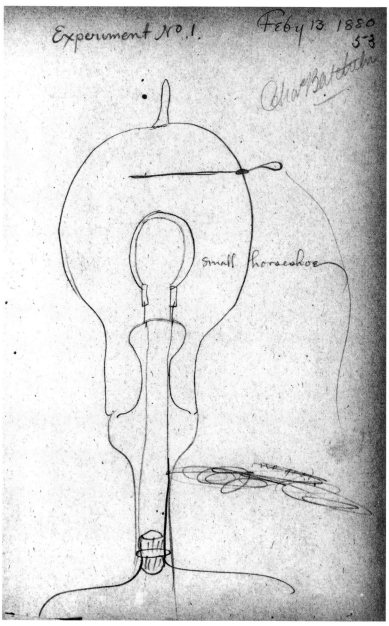

Al's notebook sketch for a lightbulb

metals, including iron, steel, and metal foil, he found that carbon was a good material for his filaments.

Al had used carbon to improve the telephone when he invented the carbon button transmitter. Carbon had also figured in his inventions in telegraphy. It was easy enough to get a good supply. When kerosene lamps burned, the black soot that formed on their glass chimneys was pure carbon. When carbon was rolled up into a filament, however, it was exceedingly fragile.

Al's laboratory team finally hit on the idea of testing ordinary thread that had been carbonized by placing it in a protective container and then subjecting it to high hcat in a furnace. On October 21, 1879, they placed a piece of carbonizcd cotton thread into a glass bulb, scaled it off, and applied electric current. This was the breakthrough that they had been waiting for! The filament burned with a steady light for thirteen and one-half hours. It had been more than a year since Al had optimistically promised to succeed in just six weeks.

Spurred on by this accomplishment, Al and his workers set out to find the best material to carbonize. They tested carbonized papcr, wood, and even carbonized fishing line and coconut shells. But the perfect filament still eluded them.

On Novcmbcr 16, 1879, there was another breakthrough. Al and his workers succeeded in creating a filament from charred paper formed into a horseshoe shape, and the results were impressive. Al decidcd the time was right to show his invention to the public. He chose New Year's Eve, 1879, as the date for his groundbreaking demonstration.

On that stormy winter night, an excited crowd of three thousand onlookers gathered in the dark to watch as the

Menlo Park facility burst into light. Along the street, too, glowing lightbulbs dispelled the darkness.

The public had never before seen anything like it. Al had succeeded in producing lighting without the glare of arc lights. His lightbulbs gave off the same gentle glow as gaslights, but without their poisonous vapors or fire hazards.

People continued to visit throughout the next day. Awestruck crowds roamed through the lab until the inventor had to order it closed to the public. But he kept the outside street lamps illuminated to please the people who had traveled to Menlo Park to witness his amazing invention.

The inventor's New Year's Eve event proved that he could produce electrical lighting, but only in his laboratory and the nearby street. He wanted to make the system possible on a larger scale. His vision was to produce an entire electrical lighting industry that would be readily available to the public at a cost equal to gaslight.

In the new year, 1880, Al pushed even harder to get his Menlo Park facility to function like a real "invention factory," as he called it. Al was like the skillful conductor of an orchestra composed of many different people, all playing different instruments, but still following his instructions and under his masterful control. He assigned specific tasks to each of his assistants, and then let them work on their own for short periods. He busily checked in at every workstation, overseeing everyone's work. He had his own desk, too, and everyone in the lab knew not to disturb him when he was absorbed in his projects.

The workers at the lab kept meticulous notebooks with dates, drawings, and details, so Al was aware of everything that went on in the lab. He had a special skill for bringing out the best in his talented crew, perhaps directing one of his

A group of Al's associates gathered on the steps of the Menlo Park lab.

workers to read certain books, or suggesting to another to go in a totally different direction with his experiments.

Al's employees had deep respect, admiration, and affection for their boss. They were all well aware of the fact that he paid them to assist him in bringing his original ideas to fruition and that he expected them to follow his orders.

The entire team was set to work on inventing a new industry. They tackled the problem of bringing practical electric lighting to homes and offices. Even though the first successful lightbulbs produced a steady, warm glow, Al continued his search for an even better filament.

He told his staff that there must be something in nature that could produce a long-lasting filament. They experimented with natural materials that contained carbon, such as various types of wood. Then they switched their focus to different types of grass. Eventually, Al and his assistants tested more than six thousand different kinds of natural fibers, including hemp, jute, and even strands of hair from his assistants' beards.

Never discounting any material, Al once picked up a bamboo fan and made a filament out of a thin strip of the strong, pliable stem. Bamboo proved to be a good choice for a long-lasting filament in preliminary tests, so Al set out to study the thousands of different types of bamboo to determine which one would yield the best results.

He hired men to travel around the world and to bring back the most exotic bamboos available. One of these men, John Segredor, searched the wild swamps of Florida, where he risked being bitten by poisonous snakes. Another man explored the jungles surrounding the Amazon River in South America. Al also sent men to Japan, India, China, and other parts of Asia. Ironically, after all this, Al decided that bamboo wasn't as suitable for filaments as was tungsten, a hard metallic chemical element that can withstand high temperatures.

In addition to his work on the lightbulb, Al had also invented a new dynamo—an earlier term for what we call a generator. At that time, his new dynamo was the most powerful and efficient machine of its kind. It was a key element in Al's plan to build the world's first central power station to supply electricity to its customers.

The machine had two long cylinders that were connected to its top and bottom. Because of its odd shape, Al's workers jokingly called it the Long-Legged Mary Ann. At that time, referring to a woman's legs was considered to be in poor taste, so the dynamo was later dubbed the Long-Waisted Mary Ann, so as not to offend anyone.

The Long-Waisted Mary Ann, Al's new generator, was a key part of the plan to light up a part of New York City.

But Al needed more than working lightbulbs and a dynamo to provide the electricity to light them. He also needed wires to carry the electric current, insulation to prevent fires, and an electric meter to see how much power his customers used. Sockets, switches, and fuses also were vital in bringing Al's vision to pass. He eventually designed all of these small but important components, and by the end of 1880, he had perfected his system of electrical distribution.

A new power plant on Pearl Street provided the electricity for the New York lighting project.

SIX

Power on Pearl Street

It was the winter of 1881. Al had his lightbulb and a system of distribution. It was time to build a power plant to supply electricity to homes and offices. The staff at Menlo Park had a hard time keeping up with the demand for the necessary lightbulbs. It became apparent to Al that he would have to establish some smaller factories to produce them and the other components of his system, so he opened plants in New York City.

He began conducting more and more of his research in his New York shops. By the fall of 1882, the inventor opted to permanently close the Menlo Park facility. He preferred to conduct his experiments in the new laboratory that he established on 17th Street in New York.

Having moved his base of operations, Al chose the site of his central station. He picked a relatively inexpensive building at 255–57 Pearl Street, near the Wall Street financial district. He hoped to gain customers among the well-to-do businessowners with offices in the area, as well as some wealthy homeowners.

Al did a complete survey of the area. He found out exactly

An illustration from an 1882 Harper's Weekly *magazine shows work crews laying power lines under the city street.*

how many gas jets there were in each home and office, and he learned how frequently gas lighting was used. He knew from these figures what each customer might be willing to pay for illumination.

From the very beginning, Al planned to send the electricity through underground cables. He considered it an extra measure of safety to have the wire surrounded by earth and not subject to being knocked down in storms or by passing traffic. Al was the only one who was qualified to oversee the laying of the cables. His ideas for electric lighting had brought about so many new products that no one else understood as completely how to carry out the installation.

Finally on September 4, 1882, the Pearl Street Power Station—the first commercial power station in the United States—was ready to operate. The board of directors of the recently established Edison Electric Light Company gathered at the offices of wealthy businessman J. P. Morgan. They anxiously waited to see if Al could fulfill his promise to light houses and offices in the southern end of Manhattan.

Everyone was silent as the station engineer threw the power switch. The generator started, and power surged through wires to the many electric lamps that Al's employees had installed. Suddenly, to everyone's delight, Morgan's office was aglow. The electric power station was a success.

Edison's electric lamp could become used worldwide with the innovation of commercially distributed electricity.

The next day, a *New York Times* reporter wrote, "The light was soft and mellow, and grateful to the eye . . . without a particle of a flicker and with scarcely any heat to make the head ache." Al commented to a reporter for a local newspaper that he had achieved everything he had promised. This was true, but Al had originally boasted to reporters that he could get the job done in only six weeks. Instead, this colossal venture had taken four long years.

An exuberant Al personally visited some customers that day. One of them told Al that the light was fine, but joked that it was too bad that he couldn't light a cigar with it as he could with gaslight. Three days later, Al returned to present his surprised client with an electric cigar lighter.

More people came to appreciate the dependability of the Pearl Street station. In just a few months, the facility was lighting more than three thousand lamps for more than two hundred customers. Nearly a year later, those figures climbed to more than ten thousand lamps and about four hundred customers.

Al was also asked to install electrical systems in countries in Europe, including England and Germany. Even in Australia, some government buildings were illuminated by electric lights.

But Al's happiness was interrupted by family concerns. Al had labored long and hard on his electrical experiments in New York City. Even though he moved his family to New York, he had even less time to spend with his wife and three children. In Menlo Park, the Edison family's house had been very close to the lab. But in New York City, the family residence was farther away. Mary and the children barely saw him at all. Al kept the house in Menlo Park, but used it mostly as a summer home.

In July 1884, Al's wife, Mary, weakened and soon became bedridden at the Menlo Park house. At first, Al didn't think

The foyer (entrance hall) of the Paris Opera in France was illuminated with Edison's electric lights.

the illness was anything to worry about, but when he learned that her condition was serious, he immediately returned to Menlo Park. On August 9, 1884, Mary died, with Al at her bedside. The cause of her death is not known, but she may have contracted typhoid fever, an infectious disease. Others think that Mary may have had a brain tumor.

Since Al was often absent from his family home, it may have seemed that he had no concern for his family. But in reality he loved them deeply. He was so focused on his work, however, that he often neglected his family without realizing how much it hurt them.

Al was truly grieved by the loss of his wife. His daughter, Marion, then eleven years old, remembered her father crying so hard that he could barely get out the words to tell her that her mother had died.

With Mary's death, Al became a single father with both business and family responsibilities. Mary's mother looked after his two sons, while Marion attended a boarding school in New York. Al had previously spent little time with his

Mary Stilwell Edison in 1883, the year before she died

daughter, but, stunned by his wife's death, the inventor grew closer to Marion, whom he still called Dot.

He treated Dot to fancy restaurants, the opera, and the theater. He allowed her to sit in on company board meetings. He accompanied her on short trips to Menlo Park. One night, he played ball with her after supper. He wrote in his diary that this was the first time that he ever tried to play catch, and that it nearly broke his little finger.

A few months after his wife's death, Al was back, busy as ever, in his New York City laboratory. Yet he found time to help Marion with her homework, and he even let her assist him in the lab. She sometimes took notes when her father was working on experiments. Al doodled in one of his work notebooks about "Dot Edison angel Miss Marion Edison Sweetest of all."

At age thirty-seven and a widower, wealthy and famous, Al was considered one of the most eligible bachelors around. Some of his friends scrambled to parade a long line of young beauties before him.

In 1885, Ezra Gilliland, an old friend who had recently become a business associate of Al, introduced him to a young lady named Mina Miller, whom Al had met only briefly a few months before. This intelligent, beautiful nineteen-year-old was the daughter of inventor Lewis Miller. She was an educated and sophisticated young woman and had just returned from a trip to Europe when she met Al this second time.

A few months later, Al wrote in his diary that he happened to see a woman who reminded him of Mina. He noted that he became so absorbed in thinking about the stunning young woman that he wasn't aware of an oncoming streetcar, and he nearly got run over. "If Mina interferes much more will have to take out an accident policy," he wrote.

Mina Miller, nineteen, was educated and sophisticated, the daughter of an educator and inventor.

Then, in August 1885, Al went on a trip with a group of people including his friend Ezra Gilliland and his wife Lillian. Mina Miller was also invited along. The journey lasted less than a week, and the party stopped in New York State and in the White Mountains of New Hampshire.

Since Al was greatly hard of hearing, he suggested to Mina that he teach her Morse code so they could tap out their conversations on each other's hands. She agreed and quickly learned the code.

One month later, Al saw Mina again with a group of friends. Surrounded by people, Al managed to secretly ask Mina to marry him by tapping out his proposal in Morse code on her hand. She tapped back, "Yes."

Al then formally received permission from Mina's father, and a wedding date was set. On the afternoon of February 24, 1886, the couple exchanged vows at Mina's parents' house in Akron, Ohio. Friends and family attended. Al, overjoyed to be marrying the refined, intelligent woman, even donned a tuxedo, a far cry from his usual stained work clothes.

Al and Mina left the party to take a train to Cleveland, Ohio. Ten days later, after stopping in several states along the way, the couple arrived in Fort Myers, Florida. Al had previously purchased some property there and had had a house built on it. The Gillilands and Al's daughter, Marion, joined them at the house.

The inventor's daughter must have been happy to spend time with her father, even if she had to share him with his new bride. Marion was understandably resentful of Mina, a young woman who was not much older than herself. Her relationship with Al's young wife continued to be shaky in the years to come.

After the honeymoon in Florida, Al took Mina to their new home. He had bought a large Victorian mansion

Al purchased Glenmont, a mansion in West Orange, New Jersey, to be the new family home.

surrounded by thirteen and a half acres of property in West Orange, New Jersey. The mansion, known as Glenmont, was located on a hill and commanded a sweeping view of the countryside. Al bought the mansion complete with artwork and furniture thrown into the bargain. The twenty-three rooms included a huge dining room where the Edisons held dinners for up to thirty people and a den where Al invited his male guests to smoke afterward.

The second floor featured a living room, family bedrooms, and guest rooms. There was a third-floor wing for the Edisons' servants. Mina soon learned how to manage her staff in order to keep the huge mansion running smoothly. She felt that it was her duty to make Al's home life as comfortable as possible so he could continue his work.

Al returned to his many experiments. Because his laboratory in New York City was about two hours away from home, he made plans for a new, well-equipped lab in New Jersey, just a short walk from Glenmont.

Edison was photographed at work in his new chemical room at the laboratory complex in West Orange.

SEVEN

Lights! Camera! Action!

Although Al had been extremely attentive to Mina during their courtship and honeymoon, his work once again took precedence over his personal life. By the end of 1887, the West Orange, New Jersey, lab was open, with nearly one thousand employees in five buildings. Al drew up a huge list of products that he wanted to work on.

He stocked this lab with an immense variety of materials, joking that he owned everything "from an elephant's hide to the eyeballs of a United States senator." Although the last item was certainly not part of the lab's supplies, Al did buy items as unusual as peacock tails, porcupine quills, bulls' horns, and walrus hides.

One of the first things that he did at the new lab was to begin work to improve the phonograph. Al said that of all his inventions, he loved the phonograph the best. During the next four years, he received more than eighty patents—government protection for inventions and designs—for the various improvements of his original design.

Al later created a project to delight children. Three thousand red-haired dolls dressed in dainty blue outfits and black

The Edison talking doll, left, with a close-up of the phonograph mechanism, right.

patent leather shoes went on sale. Each doll had a miniature phonograph inside. When a small crank was turned, the doll recited nursery rhymes. Al soon stopped selling the toys, though, because the fragile mechanisms inside often broke down, and customers complained about the dolls' unpleasant voices.

Another project led to an entirely new field of entertainment: the motion picture industry. As early as 1887, Al had begun to think about a possible new invention that, he said, "should do for the eye what the phonograph does for the ear." There had already been attempts by others at creating the illusion of motion in pictures, and the first breakthrough had come in 1878.

British photographer Eadweard Muybridge was hired by California politician Leland Stanford to help him win a bet. Stanford was convinced that running horses at one point have all four hooves off the ground. An acquaintance disagreed, and they bet a large sum of money on this issue. To settle the dispute, Muybridge set up a series of cameras attached to wires. As a horse galloped past these wires, it set off the cameras. The result was a series of photographs of the running horse. These photos proved that Stanford was correct.

Muybridge's series photography led to his invention of a simple projecting machine, the zoopraxiscope. This machine projected a series of Muybridge's still photographs of a moving object, giving the impression of movement to the viewer.

The photographer paid a visit to Al in February 1888 and suggested the possibility of combining Al's phonograph with his photo series. By October Al had filed a notice with the United States Office of Patents and Trademarks stating that he was working on the concept of talking pictures.

Part of the series of famous photographs Eadweard Muybridge took to settle a bet. Muybridge later invented a projector that gave the impression of movement to his images.

Just as Al was beginning to think about this new invention, Mina gave birth to their first child, Madeleine, on May 31, 1888. Although Al wasn't home very much, Madeleine later described her father as the type of man who would wake her up in the middle of the night to show her a spectacular sky lit up by lightning during a raging thunderstorm. He also shared the beauty of a rainbow with his daughter, and she recalled how he played the board game Parcheesi according to his own rules. "Now there was an invention for you!" she once commented.

But Al's first love was always his work. He put together a small research team headed by employee W. K. L. Dickson, who was also a photographer. Al's original plan was to use a series of tiny pictures wound around a cylinder in a continuous spiral. The viewer would look through a microscope to see the illusion of motion. Early subjects consisted of very simple movements like the wave of a hand.

By early 1889, Dickson and his team achieved this objective. But these early attempts produced only an inconsistent, jerky illusion of motion. There were white streaks, scratches, and dots on the pictures, as well. The sound part of this experiment was not working, either.

Later that year, Al attended an exhibition in Paris, France, and heard about a new type of camera invented by Étienne-Jules Marey. The French scientist designed his special camera—which looked something like a rifle—to shoot pictures on a roll of paper film. Al was very interested, and the gracious Marey spoke at length with him.

When Al returned to his lab, inspired by the work of Marey, he took his motion picture research in a different direction. He went back to some earlier ideas that he had, but did not get around to pursuing. He experimented with a camera using a roll of film like Marey's, but with small holes on the side. The camera had a small wheel with sprockets—little "teeth"—that fit into the holes in the strip of film and moved it along. Tape with similar holes had been used in the automatic telegraph, and Al never wasted any knowledge gained in his other projects.

Al became involved with other inventions and had Dickson stop his experiments. But almost a year later, Al asked Dickson to return to motion picture research, and this time, he supplied a larger team. Al kept an eye on the invention's development, and he gave his work team suggestions on the best ways to proceed.

During this time, Mina and Al's first son, Charles, was born on August 3, 1890, in the master bedroom at Glenmont. Although again happy to be a father, Al was soon back at work. Eventually, the motion picture team at the lab devised a camera called the Kinetograph, as well as a viewer, the Kinetoscope, a tall pine box with a peephole for one person at a time to view movies.

Edison's first motion picture camera, the Kinetograph, used strips of film to create smoother movement.

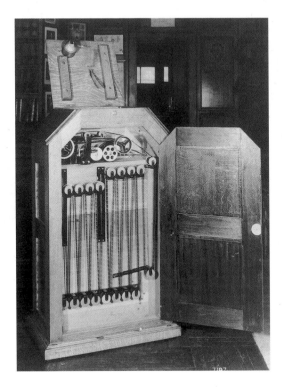

The Kinetoscope enabled a viewer to see the moving pictures through a peephole.

George Eastman's invention of celluloid film aided Al's group's work. This strong, flexible material enabled them to get sharper images on the film, which could be moved more quickly through the camera to create a smoother sense of motion.

On May 20, 1891, Al gave a private demonstration at a luncheon at Glenmont hosted by Mina for some local women. The women went to Al's laboratory and, one at a time, stepped up to the Kinetoscope's peephole. They were treated to a movie lasting less than thirty seconds. Dickson was the "star." He looked straight at the viewer, bowed, and tipped his hat. The audience was delighted.

After the preliminary demonstration, Al decided that it would soon be time to exhibit his new inventions to the

Workers at the West Orange lab built this film studio, the Black Maria, in which to make early motion pictures.

public. Instead of selling Kinetoscopes, Al rented them out so he could control the product and the profits.

Al wanted to be ready with a number of different movies to show to audiences, so in 1893, he constructed the first motion picture studio ever built. Dubbed the Black Maria, it measured about twenty-five by thirty feet. The windowless structure had black walls inside and out. The black background made actors stand out sharply on the film. The roof of the studio was partially retractable, and the entire building could swing around on a circular track. Since early motion picture film needed strong natural light, the entire studio could be moved to follow the position of the Sun.

Most of the films shot there lasted less than twenty seconds. Sometimes Al's workers were recruited as actors. Employee Fred Ott simply stood before the camera and

Patrons looked through the viewer at the top of the Kinetoscope to see the movie. This version had sound that could be listened to through the earphones.

sneezed. At other times, Al hired celebrities like heavyweight boxing champion Gentleman Jim Corbett and sharpshooter Annie Oakley.

On April 14, 1894, the first Kinetoscope parlor opened on Broadway in New York City. This was the beginning of commercial movies. The public paid twenty-five cents for a ticket that entitled them to view five movies, or fifty cents to see ten of the mini-films.

The New York parlor was so successful that others were installed in Chicago, Atlantic City, Washington, D.C., and other cities. They also were popular abroad in England, France, Germany, and other countries.

Some of the films created controversy. When a dancer named Carmencita demonstrated high kicks and ended her short film appearance with a revealing cartwheel, some viewers were shocked. Another mini-film showed a man and woman in the first-ever cinematic kiss. This caused a minor scandal, and the film instantly became popular.

By 1895 machines for projecting motion pictures onto a screen had already been invented by the Lumière brothers in France, and by others in England and Germany. The American public wanted something more exciting than peephole viewing. They were ready for movies that entire audiences could see on a large screen. In the United States, Thomas Armat and C. Francis Jenkins worked together to produce a motion picture projector called the Phantoscope. Al, believing that the public was happy with his box viewers, hadn't done research on such a device.

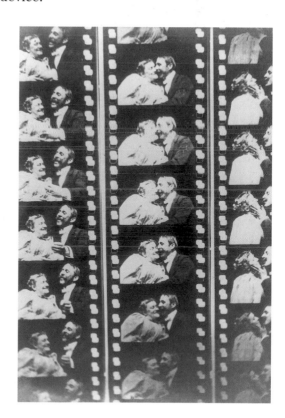

The scandalous First Kiss, *1896*

Impressed by Armat and Jenkins's Phantoscope and eager to meet the demands of the moviegoing audience, Al secured the manufacturing rights to these projectors. He changed the name to the Edison Vitascope, a move advantageous to both parties. Al was able to present a successful projector to the public, and Armat and Jenkins were able to take advantage of Al's widely respected name.

On April 23, 1896, the first commercial motion picture projector in the United States was demonstrated to an eager audience at Koster & Bial's Music Hall on 34th Street and Broadway in New York City, the present-day site of Macy's Department Store. A promotional brochure assured viewers that the Edison Vitascope was "astonishing" and "thrills the nerves."

Audiences watching motion on the big screen were astounded. Among the five short movies shown that night was *Rough Sea at Dover,* which merely presented waves rolling in and striking a pier in England. But this presentation of ocean waves was such a hit that it was shown several times that night.

Al had captured the hearts of the audience, but there would be plenty of competition in the future. Just two months after his New York showing, the Lumière brothers gave the American premiere of their own movies, shot and projected by their own inventions.

Al's production company continued working. The short novelty films evolved into longer films with stories to tell. In 1903 Al's employee Edwin S. Porter made *The Great Train Robbery,* one of the first westerns. There are heart-stopping chase scenes and some early special effects. The concluding shot shows a close-up of one of the "bad guys," who aims his gun at the audience and shoots.

The Great Train Robbery, *a longer film with a story line, was one of the first Westerns.*

But Al could never stay interested in just one invention for very long. His far-ranging imagination and capacity for hard work always led him into other fields. By the early 1900s, he had embarked on many other projects that meant more to him than producing movies. Eventually, he sold all of his motion picture interests. Al was the inventive genius who laid the groundwork for a new entertainment industry, but he left its further development to the many producers who would follow in his footsteps.

An Edison family portrait

EIGHT

Batteries and Concrete Houses

On July 10, 1898, Al and Mina's third child, Theodore, was born at Glenmont. Although Al had only played a minor role in raising his children with Mary, he was more attentive to the children of his second marriage. Mina came from a family background that stressed education. Al had virtually no formal education, and he firmly believed in self-taught knowledge. His daughter from his first marriage, Marion, once said, "My father's idea of my education was that I shouldn't have any. Or, at any rate, that I should get it by reading everything . . . as he did."

But Mina seemed to have had the upper hand in her own children's upbringing. She hired a French governess for them and made sure that her children attended fine private schools. Each winter the whole family traveled to Fort Myers to enjoy the warm Florida weather from the end of February until the middle of April.

Al's daughter Madeleine knew about her father's softer side. He detested parties, and it seemed that Mina was always

Edison had become famous for his many inventions, developed in long hours at his laboratories. But his children with second wife, Mina, remembered a man who spent some touching moments with them, too.

inviting people over to their home. Madeleine realized that her father seemed to suffer from convenient bouts of "indigestion" that started just before Mina's parties and seemed to miraculously disappear as soon as the last guests had left.

On one occasion, after Al told Mina that he was too sick to attend a party and took to his bed, Madeleine knocked on his bedroom door. She complained to her father that she, her brother Charles, and their cousin weren't allowed to go downstairs for the festivities. Even though she was fourteen years old, the party was strictly for adults.

Her father smiled and said, "We'll have a party of our own." He rang for his butler and asked for a bottle of champagne to be brought to his room immediately. The cork was popped and the bubbly champagne was poured. Al let his happy young visitors take their first few sips of champagne as they crowded around him on his bed.

Most days at home, after a nap and dinner, Al went upstairs and read up on his latest projects, writing down any new ideas as they came to him. At times Al would stay up reading until 5:00 A.M., take a short rest, and then rise at 7:30 A.M. to get ready for his long day at the lab. His son Charles called their home his father's "thought bench" and referred to the lab as the "work bench."

Every so often, Al would involve the whole family in doing his research. He would give them assignments to look up specific topics in the extensive home reference library. Everyone was instructed to put slips of paper in the books to mark passages dealing with the project Al was working on. Later he would collect the books and read everything that was marked.

One of the projects that Al was involved in during the early 1900s was a new kind of battery. In 1799 an Italian scientist named Alessandro Volta created the first battery. A battery is a device that changes chemical energy into electrical energy. These early batteries could only be used until the chemicals inside were used up. In 1859 French scientist Gaston Planté invented the first rechargeable storage battery. But the early storage batteries were very heavy and expensive to produce. Al wanted to invent a rechargeable battery that would be lighter, more powerful, and cheaper to make.

It took ten years to develop a battery that satisfied Al. As he once said, "I never allow myself to become discouraged under any circumstances." He told a disappointed worker who was frustrated by unsuccessful experiments, "We sometimes learn a lot from our failures if we have put into the effort the best thought and work we are capable of."

Al developed his storage batteries to power electric cars. If the batteries could be sold at a reasonable price, he thought, this might make electric cars more attractive to consumers

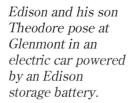

Edison and his son Theodore pose at Glenmont in an electric car powered by an Edison storage battery.

than cars powered by gasoline. Al and his workers performed more than ten thousand experiments before he was satisfied with the final product.

Even though Al achieved his objective with the storage battery, it was not enough to boost sales of electric cars. Automobile pioneer Henry Ford developed his gasoline-powered Model T car in 1908. Ford's car was a high-quality vehicle available at low cost. Electric cars couldn't compete with it, and their sales declined.

Although Al's storage battery wasn't used for his original purpose, it was still successful in supplying portable electricity for submarines, miners' lamps, and electric trucks. The batteries were also used for many years to power streetcars in New York City.

While Al was experimenting, he sometimes took his young son Charles to the lab with him. On one occasion,

Charles grew tired and Al said he could just go to sleep anywhere. At two o'clock in the morning, Al and his employees were still working, and Mina went to the lab to look for her son when he didn't return that night. She was appalled to find her child sleeping on the floor. Al just commented that no one would step on him.

When Al spit on the floor, Mina, with her refined background, offered to buy her husband a spittoon—a receptacle to spit into. He replied that he didn't need one. The floor was the best spittoon there was, he said, since you never missed when you spit onto it.

At the same time that he was working on the storage battery, Al had, as usual, many other projects going on. He became interested in manufacturing Portland cement. This is a fine gray powder that is one of the principal ingredients in

Mina learned how to deal with a husband who was a creative genius.

The long kilns developed by Edison for manufacturing cement were in use in 1942, as this photo shows, and they are still in use.

making concrete. This material was becoming very popular for construction.

Al also invented a new kiln—an oven—for use in manufacturing the cement. Because Al wanted a kiln that was able to produce larger amounts of cement than ever before, he developed one that was twice as long as any of the existing models. This type of long kiln is still in use. Al's Portland cement business became one of the major producers of the material in the United States. It even provided the building material for the construction of New York's Yankee Stadium, one of the most famous ballparks in the country.

Despite its popularity, the cement company wasn't as profitable as Al had hoped. Then he hit upon the idea of creating poured concrete houses to increase the demand for his building material. These structures would be quick and easy to build and relatively cheap. He devised an entire system of cast-iron molds that could be bolted together.

The liquid concrete was poured through the top of the molds and slowly seeped through them to the bottom, forming an entire house—all in one large piece. This included the roof, all the walls and floors, stairs, chimneys, and even bathtubs, all made of concrete. The molds were designed so that the layout of the house could be styled according to individual tastes.

It took just six hours to pour the concrete, and then six days for the substance to harden. Then workers added doors, windows, plumbing, heating, and electricity. But despite the low cost and the attractive look of these houses, they never caught on, and eventually, Al abandoned the project.

Al returned to his work on the phonograph. His records were still made in the form of cylinders, but he had

The all-concrete house that Al invented never became popular.

a lot of competition from companies like the Victor Talking Machine Company, which produced disk records. These disks were easier to store than Al's cylinders, and the public liked the louder volume the flat records produced.

So Al set to work on perfecting disk records and on improving his phonograph. It took the better part of five years. At one point, in the fall of 1911, Al gathered a team of his workers that was jokingly referred to as the Insomnia Squad, because they worked so hard and barely slept. During one period of intensive experimenting, they spent an almost uninterrupted five weeks concentrating on the phonograph. They worked and slept at the lab. Al went

The Insomnia Squad stops work to eat a meal.

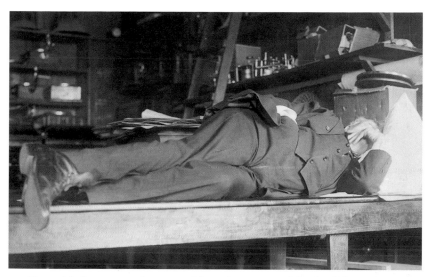

Al could sleep anywhere, and he often napped in the lab on chairs, desks, and even tables.

home only a few times during this period to change his disheveled clothes.

Al took short naps in the lab, or sometimes even curled up on his large desk. Food and drink were brought in so no one would have to stop working. No one shaved during this time.

The lab's team at last developed the Edison Disc [sic] Phonograph, which played the round, flat records popular with the public. The disk records were made from a new material developed in the Edison labs. The records were billed as "practically unbreakable," and they provided high-quality sound reproduction. The Edison phonograph was redesigned and used a diamond needle that made the records sound even louder and clearer than before.

Over the next few years, more improvements were made on other parts of the phonograph. But on December 9, 1914, a wooden shed at the lab, which was used to store highly

In December 1914, a fire destroyed the phonograph works at the West Orange lab.

flammable motion picture film, caught fire. The flames quickly spread to nearby buildings that contained large stores of chemicals and tanks filled with alcohol. These fueled the fire, and the laboratory complex was ablaze in a short time. One of Al's workers died and twelve firemen were injured.

It took twenty-four hours to subdue the fire. Al was sixty-eight years old, a time when most people have already retired from business. Yet his spirit had not been destroyed in the blaze. Even before the fire was out, he was busy planning how he would rebuild his lab complex. He told his son Charles, "We'll have a much better plant after we get through. We've swept away all the old shacks, and now we can have a good plant."

Al received a pleasant surprise on New Year's Day, 1915. Just three weeks after the fire had devastated the lab, his workers presented him with the first phonograph produced after some of their machinery had been restored. It was proof that Al's optimism was stronger than the flames that destroyed his buildings. His attitude inspired his employees to continue working in the face of this tragedy.

Edison, right, and an associate discuss plans in the West Orange lab.

NINE

A World at War

In July 1914, World War I began. The United States did not officially enter the war until 1917, but even before that, Americans could feel the effects. Germany, Austria-Hungary, and several other countries composed the Central Powers. They were at war with the Allies: England, France, Russia, and other nations.

In an effort to win the war, the British navy sent ships to close or blockade Germany's ports. The British wanted to make sure that Germany could not export supplies or obtain raw materials that would help the German war effort.

Because Al and many other manufacturers relied on German chemicals and other raw materials to produce some of their products, the European conflict caused problems for them in the United States. Al always bought potash for his storage batteries from Germany. When Germany was prevented from exporting goods to the United States, Al found ways to use other materials that were more readily available instead.

Al thought that he might have to abandon his entire phonograph business because he needed some chemicals, such as carbolic acid, that he could not buy in the United States. He immediately went to work to find a way to produce his own carbolic acid. In his usual determined way, Al studied everything that he could find on the subject of creating a carbolic acid plant. He put together three teams of workers, and they took turns, working around the clock. After just eighteen days, a carbolic acid plant was in production. After only one month, the plant produced more than one ton of the chemical each day. Just a few months later, that amount increased to six tons a day. Al eventually also produced other chemicals that he formerly bought from Germany, and it saved his business and those of other manufacturers who began to buy their supplies from him.

The United States was still not directly involved in the war. But on May 7, 1915, the Germans sank the *Lusitania,* a British passenger ship. Among those who died in the attack

The sinking of the Lusitania *by a German submarine helped convince the United States to join the Allies in World War I.*

were more than one hundred American civilians. A few weeks later, a reporter from the *New York Times* interviewed Al and asked him what course of action he thought the United States should take. The inventor answered that, among other things, the country should prepare for possible war by constructing a large number of submarines and other vessels.

When the Secretary of the Navy, Josephus Daniels, read Al's ideas in the newspaper, he decided to contact him. In July 1915, Daniels wrote Al a letter in which he explained his idea of creating a group of important people who would give advice to the navy. He asked Al to join the proposed group.

Al answered that he would be proud to serve. In the fall of 1915, the group, known as the Naval Consulting Board of the United States, met, and Al served as its first chairman and

Edison, left, was appointed to the Naval Consulting Board of the United States by the Secretary of the Navy.

later as president of the board. For the next several years, Al left his other experiments behind and put most of his energy into working with the Naval Consulting Board.

Among the many experiments he carried out were the development of improved torpedoes, underwater searchlights, and a telephone system for ships. One of his greatest concerns was how to prevent the navy's ships from being damaged or destroyed by torpedoes launched by German submarines.

Al devised a device that would allow a ship to change its course quickly to get out of the way of an oncoming torpedo. He also came up with a very practical way to keep ships from being sunk. He studied the available information on the ships that had been sunk by the Germans. To his great surprise, he learned that these ships had been following the same routes that they had been using before the war began. The inventor also noted that most of the destruction came during the daytime. By suggesting that the ships change their courses and times, Al proposed a simple effective plan to save ships and lives.

During his time with the Naval Consulting Board, Al came up with forty-five inventions or strategic plans. To his great disappointment, the navy never put any of his plans or inventions to use. He felt that suggestions from a civilian were resented by navy personnel.

Al continued to work hard for his country, but when he was in his late sixties, he allowed himself some brief relaxation from his workdays, which often lasted from sixteen to twenty hours. In 1916, at the age of sixty-nine, he began going on annual camping trips with his friends, automobile manufacturer Henry Ford, rubber manufacturer Harvey S. Firestone, and naturalist John Burroughs. On one of their excursions, they even took President Warren G. Harding with them.

President Warren Harding, second from right, *joined Henry Ford,* left, *Al,* second from left, *and Harvey Firestone,* right, *on one of their camping trips, August 1921.*

On their first trip, they drove one thousand miles from New Jersey through the Adirondack Mountains in New York State and then back through Vermont. Al provided four tents and even supplied one of his storage batteries to light up the campsite and the tents. His one hard and fast rule was that no one be allowed to shave on these trips.

Even though Al spent most of his life experimenting indoors, he was actually a great lover of nature. He took pleasure in collecting wildflowers, and he would closely observe the many birds and other varieties of wildlife around the campsite. He studied streams and speculated on how their power could be harnessed. But he also was the only man in the group who took books with him.

Everyone on the camping trips enjoyed Al's great sense of humor and his ability to tell stories. They would wonder

Naturalist John Burroughs, second from right, *was a regular member of Al's camping group.*

how this man could be telling jokes one minute and then the next be curled up under the nearest tree to take a short nap. Sometimes the party would sit around the campfire at night and ask Al questions. His friends were amazed at the way the inventor could rattle off one chemical formula after another from memory.

Al continued to work for the government until January 1921, when the Naval Research Laboratory was established in

Washington with naval officers in charge. Al had suggested that civilians should run the lab, but this suggestion was declined.

Returning to his own lab, Al continued with his experiments. That year a small controversy arose about the methods that the great inventor used to choose his employees. For many years, he had given prospective workers a questionnaire that was made up of more than one hundred questions. He would base his opinions on whether or not to hire someone by how well they scored.

In 1921 some New York newspapers published "The Edison Questionnaire," and a debate ensued over whether the inventor was being fair by judging people by this test. Some of the questions were: "What countries bound France?" "Where is the River Volga?" and "Is Australia greater than Greenland in area?" Critics thought that the test wasn't a good measure of a person's intelligence.

Al found that most of the job applicants who took the test failed miserably. He blamed the poor scores on the education system of his day. His opinion was that if children between the ages of twelve and seventeen weren't taught an interest in learning, they would have a hard time succeeding in the future.

Al told those who disagreed with his testing methods that he didn't care whether or not someone knew where Napoleon was born. That information was totally unimportant to Al. What he was interested in, he said, was a test of a prospective employee's memory.

He once told the editor of *Scientific American,* the respected magazine, that he thought one of the most important qualifications for a good worker was a good memory. He said that just having a good memory didn't necessarily mean that the person would be the best one for the job. But if a man

didn't have a good memory, then he would lack the first qualification for it.

He added, "The only way I know to test a man's memory is to find out how much he has remembered and how much he has forgotten." It was not important if a man knew the capital of Nevada, but if a prospective employee had once learned what it was and then forgot it, the inventor said, then he would worry about giving such a man a job.

Al had an incredible memory, according to workers who were close to him. For instance, one day he arrived early in the morning to look over one of his factories. He walked around and surveyed the machinery and the workings of the plant, all without taking notes. He left in the late afternoon, and when he got home, he took out a notebook and began writing down his observations. He made a list of six hundred items that he had noted. He said that a good memory was partly a gift and partly something that could be learned.

Edison said that he owed part of his success to his excellent memory, and he looked for employees with the same power to remember things.

Al and his family spent most winters at the house he had had built in Fort Myers, Florida.

TEN

An Aging Genius

$\mathbf{A}$s the years passed, Al's mind remained as sharp as ever, but his body understandably began to grow weak with age. In January 1923, when he was seventy-seven years old and in Fort Myers, Florida, for his usual winter stay, he contracted a severe cold. Weakened by his condition, he decided to stay in the pleasant climate until May before heading back to New Jersey with Mina.

Back in New Jersey, his general health began to deteriorate. He began sleeping longer hours, unusual for the man who would sometimes stay awake all night to complete experiments. He found he had to cut down on his hours in the laboratory. He gradually regained his strength, but by the winter of 1924, he was feeling weak again. Then he lost a great deal of weight over the next few years. In 1926, his physician, Dr. Hubert S. Howe, diagnosed Al with an ulcer—a sore in the digestive tract. It was painful for the inventor to eat, and eventually Al came to the conclusion that his condition would get better if he drank only milk. This stopped some of the pain, but it is doubtful that Al's restricted diet was good for his general health.

To make matters worse, Al disliked the taste of water, and he could only be persuaded to drink it if it had been flavored with peppermint. Dr. Howe said that his patient needed to drink large amounts of water to flush out his kidneys, but Al was not cooperative, and his kidney problems progressed.

In addition, Al had been diagnosed with diabetes. His doctor said that Al must have had the disease for many years, but that it had become more serious over time. The doctor gave him insulin to control this condition.

In 1926 Al managed to work on his last major project. For several years, he had toyed with the idea of finding a new, domestic source of rubber. This strong, elastic material is made by processing latex, the milky white liquid obtained from rubber trees, which grow in the tropics. The major supplier of

In 1926 Edison began to investigate new, domestic sources of rubber so there would be a steady supply in the event that sources overseas became unavailable. In this photograph, Edison jots notes on his findings.

Al, with Mina at his side, cuts the cake at his eightieth birthday party in 1927.

rubber at the time was Great Britain. That nation obtained rubber from its plantations in British tropical colonies. Al's longtime friends Ford and Firestone agreed to finance Al's experiments when Great Britain raised rubber prices. They formed the Edison Botanic Research Corporation.

Al planted trees, shrubs, and vines on nine acres of his land at Fort Myers, for use in his experiments. Many of the plants naturally produced latex, the same milky liquid found in rubber trees, but in much smaller quantities.

Though older and weaker, Al gave all his mental energy to this project. He went about his research in his usual thorough way. He hired a number of employees to collect plants in several states in the South. He also received help from the New York Botanic Gardens and the Arnold Arboretum in

Edison and an associate examine a goldenrod plant, a possible source of rubber.

Boston. Al even collected plants himself when he was in New Jersey. By 1929 he and his helpers had amassed a collection of more than fifteen thousand plants.

Al found that the most promising plant he tested was goldenrod, a long-stemmed plant with clusters of small golden flowers, and he planned to extract the rubbery liquid from goldenrod plants the following year. Then rubber prices fell, so the reason for developing domestic rubber was gone.

On October 20, 1928, Al was awarded the Congressional Gold Medal, the highest award given to civilians in the United States. The government bestowed the medal on the inventor for his lifelong contributions to science. The face of the gold medal shows Al in profile, while the back inscription reads, "He Illuminated the Path of Progress by His Inventions."

The medal was awarded to Al at his laboratory in New Jersey. The entire celebration was broadcast on the radio so fans around the country could follow the proceedings. Calvin Coolidge was then the president of the United States. His message to the inventor to continue to inspire "those who will carry forward your torch" was heard in all parts of the country.

A few years after receiving the Congressional Gold Medal, Al's health hit a new low. By the end of September 1931, in addition to his generally weakened condition, Al's life-long hearing problems worsened to the point that he could only understand Mina's familiar voice. His eyesight also

Al, center, *with friends Henry Ford,* left, *and Harvey Firestone,* right, *early in 1931*

dimmed. Dr. Howe said that even near the very end, Al continued to ask many questions about the causes of his condition. It was as if his physical problems interested him in the same way as his laboratory experiments. Eventually, his strength failed him altogether, and he sank into a coma.

In the early morning of October 18, 1931, Mina and her children, Madeleine, Charles, and Theodore, along with their spouses, quietly gathered around Al's bed. Alongside them were the inventor's children by his first marriage to Mary Stilwell—Marion, Thomas Alva Jr., and William.

Just before he died, Al seemed to regain consciousness for one brief moment. With a dreamy smile on his face, he looked upward and exclaimed, "It is very beautiful over there." Then he quietly and peacefully passed away at 3:24 A.M. in the same large bed where Mina had given birth to their three children. Slowly and silently, all the relatives left Al's deathbed, but his faithful wife Mina, grief-stricken at her beloved husband's death, stayed at his side until she was gently led away to her room.

The whole country mourned the passing of the great inventor. Al's body was laid in a casket and placed in the library of the West Orange laboratory for two days. Thousands of mourners came to pay their respects.

A private service was held at Glenmont. Mina and her family welcomed some of Al's close friends, including the Firestones and the Fords. They were joined by the wife of Herbert Hoover. The president had expressed his apologies for not being able to attend because of a political meeting. In a great nationwide show of respect for the inventor, President Hoover requested that everyone in the United States observe a moment of darkness. At 10 P.M. Eastern Standard Time, every light in the entire country was shut off. Even

Crowds in West Orange, New Jersey, wait to pay their last respects to Edison, who died on October 18, 1931.

the illuminated torch on the Statue of Liberty was extinguished as the nation observed one minute of silence and darkness.

The world had lost one of its greatest inventors. He was a practical man with a phenomenal memory and an imagination that enabled him to envision machines no one had ever dreamed of before. In eighty-four years, Thomas Alva Edison had amassed a total of 1,093 patents in the United States, a record that no one has broken to this day. Certainly the world would be a very different place if it had not been for the brilliance and the hard work of the man who said, "Genius is 1 per cent inspiration and 99 per cent perspiration."

As the inventor of the Age of Electricity, Al had brought the world out of its darkness. In all, he was responsible for the growth of three separate industries. He pioneered commercial electric power. He created the music industry with his invention of the phonograph. He revolutionized the entertainment industry with his development of motion pictures. He also contributed to mass communication with his extensive work in telegraphy and the telephone, and he gave the world a practical storage battery.

When Thomas Alva Edison died, George Eastman, who perfected the celluloid film that was instrumental in the success of Al's motion picture experiments, said, "The world has lost one of the greatest men of all time."

The mayor of New York City, James Walker, noted, "Whether we consider the incandescent light, the phonograph or any of the other myriad things we daily use in the fields of light, sound and electrical energy, Edison's inventive influence is felt."

But perhaps Albert Einstein, the Nobel Prize–winning physicist, expressed it best. He realized that the great contributions of Thomas Alva Edison left a responsibility in the hands of those who would follow him. Einstein said, "An inventive spirit has filled . . . our existence with bright light [and] . . . a mission is placed in our hands. For to the new generation falls the task of finding the way for the right use of the gift given to us. Only if it solves this task will the new generation be worthy of its inheritance and become really happier than former generations."

"Whether we consider the incandescent light, the phonograph or any of the other myriad things we daily use in the fields of light, sound and electrical energy, Edison's inventive influence is felt."
—New York Mayor James Walker, speaking of Edison, above, and his many contributions to science

IMPORTANT DATES IN THOMAS EDISON'S LIFE

1847 Edison is born in Milan, Ohio, on February 11.

1854 The Edison family moves to Port Huron, Michigan.

1859 Edison gets a job as a candy butcher. He sets up a chemistry lab and a printing press on the train.

1863 TO 1867 Edison works as a tramp telegraph operator in various cities of the Midwest and Canada.

1868 Edison becomes a telegraph operator for Western Union in Boston. He invents an automatic vote recorder.

1869 Edison moves to New York City, where he works for Samuel Laws's Gold and Stock Reporting Telegraph Company. He becomes a full-time inventor.

1870 Edison opens a manufacturing shop and invention lab in Newark, New Jersey.

1871 Edison devises several important improvements in stock ticker technology for Western Union. He marries Mary Stilwell, one of his employees.

1873 Daughter Marion is born.

1874 Edison invents the quadruplex telegraph for Western Union, which can transmit four messages simultaneously.

1875 Edison invents the electric pen.

1876 Son Thomas Alva Jr. is born. Edison moves to Menlo Park, New Jersey, and establishes his first full-scale research laboratory.

1877 Edison invents the carbon transmitter to improve the telephone. He invents the phonograph.

1878 Son William Leslie is born.

1879 Edison develops the lightbulb and a generator for electric lighting.

1880 Edison develops the components of his electric lighting system for commercial use.

1881 Edison opens new offices in New York City. He begins construction on the first permanent central power station, on Pearl Street.

1882 New York power station opens and provides lights to a section of New York City.

1884 Mary (Stilwell) Edison dies.

1886 Edison marries Mina Miller and moves to West Orange, New Jersey.

1887 Edison completes a new laboratory in West Orange.

1888 Daughter Madeleine is born.

1891 Edison demonstrates the Kinetoscope, the first movie viewer.

1893 Edison builds the Black Maria, his movie studio.

1894 The first Kinetoscope parlor opens to show movies to the public.

1896 Edison introduces his Vitascope, the first commercial motion picture projector in the United States.

1898 Son Theodore is born.

1899 Edison begins work on a storage battery.

1909 Edison markets his storage battery, which is used in a host of commercial applications.

1912 Edison puts his disk records on the market.

1914 Much of the West Orange factory complex is devastated by fire.

1915 Secretary of the Navy Josephus Daniels appoints Edison to head the Naval Consulting Board of the United States.

1916 Edison, Henry Ford, John Burroughs, and Harvey Firestone begin a tradition of vacationing together.

1927 Edison forms the Edison Botanic Research Corporation to develop a process for producing rubber from domestic plant substances.

1928 Edison is awarded the Congressional Gold Medal.

1931 Edison dies in West Orange, New Jersey, on October 18. The nation dims its lights for one minute on the day of his funeral.

Pronunciation Guide

Alessandro Volta   [ah-lays-SAHN-droh VOHL-tah]

André-Marie Ampère   [ahn-dray-mah-REE ahm-PER]

Black Maria   [BLAK muh-RY-uh]

Eadweard Muybridge   [EHD-werd MY-bridge]

Étienne-Jules Marey   [ay-TYEHN-zhul mah-RAY]

Gaston Planté   [gahs-TOHN plahn-TAY]

Hans Christian Oersted   [HAHNS KREE-styahn UR-stehd]

incandescence   [ihn-kan-DESS-ehnts]

Lumière   [loom-YEHR]

Milan   [MY-lihn]

Mina Miller   [MY-nah MIHL-er]

tasimeter   [ta-SIH-mih-ter]

zoopraxiscope   [ZOH-oh-PRAX-ih-skohp]

Sources

p. 12   Francis Arthur Jones, *The Life Story of Thomas Alva Edison* (New York: Grosset & Dunlap Publishers, 1907), 8.

p. 13   Dagobert D. Runes, editor, *The Diary and Observations of Thomas Alva Edison* (New York: Philosophical Library, 1948), 45.

p. 14   Ibid.

p. 33   Reese Jenkins, Robert Rosenburg, et al., *The Papers of Thomas A. Edison* (Baltimore: Johns Hopkins University Press, 1989), 1:637.

p. 35   Frank Lewis Dyer and Thomas Commerford Martin, *Edison: His Life and Inventions* (New York and London: Harper & Brothers Publishers, 1929), 132.

p. 44   Ibid., 208.

p. 52   Ibid., 297.

p. 64   Ronald W. Clark, *Edison: The Man Who Made the Future* (New York: G. P. Putnam's Sons, 1977), 139.

p. 66   Paul Israel, *Edison: A Life of Invention* (New York: John Wiley & Sons, Inc., 1998), 234.

p. 67   Runes, *The Diary and Observations of Thomas Alva Edison,* 17.

p. 71   Robert Conot, *A Streak of Luck: The Life & Legend of Thomas Alva Edison* (New York: Seaview Books, 1979), 249.

p. 72   Dyer and Martin, *Edison: His Life and Inventions,* 537.

p. 74	Madeleine Edison Sloane, souvenir program for the "Premiere Ball," for the launch of the MGM film *Edison the Man,* 1940.	p. 109	Dyer and Martin, *Edison: His Life and Inventions,* 815.
p. 83	John D. Venable, *Out of the Shadow: The Story of Charles Edison* (East Orange, NJ: Charles Edison Fund, 1978), 20.	p. 110	"Edison's Body Lies in His Laboratory," *New York Times,* October 19, 1931, 25.
		p. 112	"Tribute by Leaders in State and City," *New York Times,* October 19, 1931, 26.
p. 84	Ibid., 23.	p. 112	"Edison Is Mourned as Leader of Age," *New York Times,* October 19, 1931, 26.
p. 85	Runes, *The Diary and Observations of Thomas Alva Edison,* 43.	p. 113	"Tribute by Leaders in State and City," *New York Times,* October 19, 1931, 26.
p. 92	Venable, *Out of the Shadow,* 76.		
p. 103	Jones, *The Life Story of Thomas Alva Edison,* 324.		

Bibliography

Books

Clarke, Ronald W. *Edison: The Man Who Made the Future.* New York: G. P. Putnam's Sons, 1977.

Conot, Robert. *A Streak of Luck: The Life & Legend of Thomas Alva Edison.* New York: Seaview Books, 1979.

The DK Science Encyclopedia. New York: DK Publishing, Inc., 1998.

Dyer, Frank Lewis, and Thomas Commerford Martin. *Edison: His Life and Inventions.* New York and London: Harper & Brothers Publishers, 1929.

Gronemeyer, Andrea. *Film: An Illustrated Historical Overview.* New York: Barron's, 1998.

How Things Work. New York: Simon and Schuster, 1984.

Israel, Paul. *Edison: A Life of Invention.* New York: John Wiley & Sons, Inc., 1998.

Jenkins, Reese, Rosenburg, Robert, et. al. *The Papers of Thomas A. Edison.* Baltimore: Johns Hopkins University Press, 1989.

Jones, Francis Arthur. *The Life Story of Thomas Alva Edison.* New York: Grosset & Dunlap Publishers, 1907.

Musser, Charles. *The Emergence of Cinema: The American Screen to 1907.* Berkeley, CA: University of California Press, 1994.

Palmer, Arthur J. *Edison: Inspiration to Youth.* Milan, OH: Edison Birthplace Association, Inc., 1928.

Parkinson, David. *History of Film.* New York: Thames and Hudson, 1995.

Runes, Dagobert D., ed. *The Diary and Observations of Thomas Alva Edison.* New York: Philosophical Library, 1948.

Venable, John D. *Mina Miller Edison: Daughter, Wife and Mother of Inventors.* East Orange, NJ: Charles Edison Fund, 1987.

———. *Out of the Shadow: The Story of Charles Edison.* East Orange, NJ: Charles Edison Fund, 1978.

Articles

Edison, Thomas A. "The Phonograph and Its Future." *North American Review* 126, June 1878.

"Edison Began Experiments as Boy and Won Fame Early; Long Career Boon to World." *New York Times,* October 19, 1931, 24.

"Edison Courageous as End Approached." *New York Times,* October 19, 1931, 27.

"Edison Is Mourned as Leader of Age." *New York Times,* October 19, 1931, 26.

"Edison Is Mourned throughout the World." *New York Times,* October 19, 1931, 1.

"Edison's Body Lies in His Laboratory." *New York Times,* October 19, 1931, 25.

"Edison's New Laboratory." *Scientific American,* September 17, 1887, 184.

"Light Bulb Balked Edison for Months." *New York Times,* October 19, 1931, 25.

Sloane, Madeleine Edison. Souvenir program for the "Premiere Ball," 1940.

"A Talk with Edison." *Scientific American,* April 2, 1892, 216.

"World Made Over by Edison's Magic." *New York Times,* October 19, 1931, 25.

Edison Museums

Edison & Ford Winter Estates
2350 McGregor Boulevard, Fort Myers, FL 33901
(941) 334-7419
<http://www.edison-ford-estate.com/>

Henry Ford Museum and Greenfield Village
20900 Oakwood Boulevard, Dearborn, MI 48121
(313) 271-1620
<http://www.hfmgv.org/>

Websites

Edison After Forty
<http://americanhistory.si.edu/edison/>

Thomas A. Edison Papers
<http://edison.rutgers.edu>

Thomas Alva Edison in Menlo Park, New Jersey
<http://www.jhalpin.com/metuchen/tae/taeindex.htm>

Further Reading

Books

Adair, Gene. *Thomas Alva Edison: Inventing the Electric Age.* Oxford, England: Oxford University Press Childrens Books, 1997.
Black-and-white photos and drawings by Edison enhance this exploration of the great inventor's many gadgets. Edison's scientific principles are explained simply and carefully.

Bender, Lionel. *Eyewitness: Invention.* New York: DK Publishing, 2000.
This book is an excellent visual aide for many important inventions, including some of Edison's. The bright color photographs bring the inventions to life.

Cook, James G., and the Thomas Alva Edison Foundation. *The Thomas Edison Book of Easy and Incredible Experiments.* New York: John Wiley & Sons, 1988.
This book offers many enlightening and fun-to-do science experiments. It is a great way to experience the joy of scientific discovery.

Egan, Lorraine Hopping. *Inventors and Inventions.* New York: Scholastic, 1999.
A history of inventors—including Edison—and their work, this book also includes posters and games.

Good, Keith. *Zap It!: Exciting Electricity Activities.* Minneapolis, MN: Lerner Publications Company, 1999.
This interactive book invites readers to use readily available materials to design and make working technology projects. It includes diagrams, tips, and questions about the projects.

King, David C. *Thomas Alva Edison: The King of Inventors.* Lowell, MA: Discovery Enterprises Ltd., 1997.
Notes from Edison's journal and his personal lab notes make this biography unique. It highlights his successes and failures, many times in his own words.

Meiani, Antonella. *Light.* Minneapolis, MN: Lerner Publications Company, 1999.
How do shadows form and why do they change shape? Why can we see very little in the dark? This book, filled with experiments, answers these questions and more.

Oxlade, Chris. *Movies.* Chicago: Heinemann Library, 1997.
This book tells the history of motion pictures, from Edison to the present. The science of the camera and the film process are explained.

Parker, Steve. *Thomas Edison and Electricity.* Philadelphia: Chelsea House, 1995.
This biography covers Edison's life, highlighting his achievements on an easy-to-follow timeline.

Wulffson, Don L. *The Kid Who Invented the Trampoline: More Surprising Stories about Inventions.* New York: Dutton Books, 2001.
False teeth, parking meters, and Post-it® Notes were all invented in strange and interesting ways. Read the fun history of fifty inventions in this book and learn about more inventors like Edison who have contributed to modern-day life.

Museums and Websites

The Bakken Library and Museum
<http://www.thebakken.org/>
This educational center for the study of electricity and magnetism holds more than 2,500 scientific instruments of old. Located in Minneapolis, Minnesota, The Bakken has electrifying exhibits and workshops for young inventors.

Edison Birthplace Museum
9 Edison Drive
Milan, OH 44846
(419) 499-2135
<http://www.tomedison.org>
The Edison Birthplace Museum is located in Milan, Ohio, and has many

examples of Edison's inventions along with his documents and family mementos. If you can't make it to Ohio, the museum's website has a virtual tour and information about Edison's home town.

Edison National Historic Site
Main Street and Lakeside Avenue
West Orange, NJ 07052
(973) 736-0550
<http://www.nps.gov/edis/home.htm>
 A virtual tour of the Edison laboratories and home in West Orange, New Jersey, which is a National Historic Site, and information about how to take actual tours.

Electrical Safety World
<http://www.sce.com/site/index.html>
A tool especially for young students of science, this site showcases many different inventors who worked with energy. Learn more about Edison and those who followed in his footsteps.

Inventing Entertainment
<http://memory.loc.gov/ammem/edhtml/edhome.html>
This Library of Congress site explores the history of the Edison Company's motion pictures. It includes a history of Edison's film work as well as some digitized films to view online.

Menlo Park in Edison, New Jersey: The Birthplace of Recorded Sound
<http://www.edisonnj.org/menlopark/>
Information about and photographs of Edison's inventions at his Menlo Park laboratory, including photos of the development of the lightbulb.

Thomas Edison House
<http://www.edisonhouse.org>
Another Edison historic site is one of his homes when he was a tramp telegrapher, in Louisville, Kentucky. On display in the house are original Edison phonographs and the first home motion picture projector.

Index

arc lighting, 51
Armat, Thomas, 79–80

baggage car lab, 20, 25–26
Barker, George F., 47
Batchelor, Charles, 45
batteries, 85–86, 87
Bell, Alexander Graham, 41
Black Maria, 77
Burroughs, John, 98, 100

candy butchers, 19, 20
carbon filaments, 53, 55
carbon transmitter, 41
cars, 85–86
chemical production, 95–96
Civil War, 23, 28, 29
concrete houses, 88–89
Congressional Gold Medal,
   108–109

Dickson, W. K. L., 74, 75, 76
dynamo. *See* generator

Eastman, George, 76, 113
eclipse, 47–47
Edison, Charles (son), 75, 84, 85,
   86–87, 110
Edison, Madeleine (daughter), 74,
   83–84, 110
Edison, Marion (Dot) (daughter),
   36–37, 39, 65–66, 68, 83, 110
Edison, Mary (Stilwell) (first wife),
   36–37, 39, 40–41, 47–49, 53,
   64–65, 66
Edison, Mina (Miller) (second
   wife), 67–69, 71, 74, 75, 83–84,
   87, 109, 110
Edison, Nancy (mother), 9, 12–13,
   16, 35
Edison, Samuel Jr. (father), 9, 12

Edison, Theodore (son), 83, 86,
   110
Edison, Thomas Alva (Al):
   ancestry, 8–9; birth and
   childhood, 8–27; deafness,
   9–20, 32, 68, 109; death, 110;
   and education, 13, 83; and
   failure, 42, 53, 85, 92–93; as a
   family man, 37, 40, 47, 49, 53,
   64–65, 71, 74, 75, 83–85; and
   nature, 99; and the navy, 97–98,
   100–101; nicknames, 8, 40, 46;
   notebooks, 42–43, 54, 66, 102;
   old age, 105–110; personality,
   12, 17, 36–37, 40, 51, 52, 81, 87,
   99–100, 102; prints newspaper,
   20–21; and profit motive,
   21–22, 24–25, 34, 77, 88, 108;
   reading habits, 13–14, 15, 19,
   31, 99; siblings, 9–10; as
   telegrapher, 27, 29–34; work
   habits, 34, 37, 47, 74, 85, 90–91,
   111
Edison, Thomas Alva Jr. (son),
   36–37, 39, 65, 110
Edison, William Leslie (son), 53,
   65, 110
Edison Disc Phonograph, 91
Edison Electric Light Company,
   62–63
Edison Vitascope, 80
electrical power system, 50, 51, 58,
   62, 112; components for, 59, 62;
   in Europe, 64–65. *See also* Pearl
   Street Power Station
electricity, 7; history of, 8, 14, 51
electric pen, 35
employees, 40, 52, 56–57, 101–102

film, celluloid, 76
Firestone, Harvey S., 98, 99, 109

124

Other Titles in the Lerner Biographies Series

Agatha Christie

Alice Walker

Allan Pinkerton

Aung San Suu Kyi

Babe Didrikson Zaharias

Billie Jean King

The Brontë Family

Charles Darwin

Charlie Chaplin

Deng Xiaoping

Douglas MacArthur

Dwight D. Eisenhower

E. B. White

Ella Fitzgerald

Emily Dickinson

F. Scott Fitzgerald

The 14th Dalai Lama

Frances Hodgson Burnett

Frank Lloyd Wright

George Balanchine

Gloria Steinem

Indira Gandhi

J. M. Barrie

J. R. R. Tolkien

Jonas Salk

John Muir

Julia Morgan

L. Frank Baum

Laura Ingalls Wilder

Leonard Bernstein

Lewis Carroll

Margaret Bourke-White

Maria Montessori

Marie Curie and Her
   Daughter Irène

Marilyn Monroe

Martin Luther King, Jr.

Mother Jones

Nellie Bly

Nikola Tesla

Rachel Carson

Ray Charles

Robert Louis Stevenson

Sir Edmund Hillary

Sylvia Earle

Theodore Herzl

Photo Acknowledgments

The photographs are reproduced with the permission of: U.S. Department of the Interior, National Parks Service, Edison National Historic Site, pp. 1, 2, 9 (both), 10, 11, 13, 18, 21, 26, 27, 33, 35, 36, 37, 38, 41, 43, 44, 45, 47, 50, 52, 53 (all), 54, 57, 59, 60, 62, 65, 66, 67, 69, 70, 75, 76, 77, 78, 79, 81, 82, 84, 87, 88, 89, 90, 91, 92, 94, 97, 99, 100, 104, 106, 107, 108, 109, 111; *The Daily Graphic,* p. 6; Library of Congress, pp. 14 (LC-D416-22), 32 (LC-USZ62-93785), 72 (LC-USZ62-107099); © Bettmann/CORBIS, pp. 15, 46, 48, 63, 102; Hulton|Archive, pp. 16, 73, 96; © CORBIS, pp. 24, 31; Henry Ford Museum & Greenfield Village Research Center, p. 25; © Medford Historical Society Collection/CORBIS, p. 28; Underwood & Underwood, p. 86; Edison Institute, p. 113; © Steve Eisenberg, p. 128;

Cover: U.S. Department of the Interior, National Parks Service, Edison National Historic Site (both).

About the Author

A frequent contributor to the *New York Times,* author Linda Tagliaferro has also written for many national magazines including *Boys' Life.* Several of her books have been chosen by the Children's Book Committee at Bank Street College as Best Children's Books of the Year. Her most recent title, *Galápagos Islands,* was chosen by the National Science Teachers Association/Children's Book Council as an Outstanding Science Trade Book for Children as well as being an Honor Book for the Society of School Librarians International. Tagliaferro does frequent presentations on her books and has spoken at the New York Hall of Science. She lives in New York with her husband and son.